BIRDS OF KENYA

BIRDS OF KENYA

A Celebration

DAVE RICHARDS FRPS

HAMISH HAMILTON · LONDON

This book is dedicated to my mother and father

HAMISH HAMILTON LTD

Published by the Penguin Group
27 Wrights Lane, London W8 5TZ, England
Viking Penguin Inc., 375 Hudson Street, New York,
New York 10014, USA
Penguin Books Australia Ltd, Ringwood,
Victoria, Australia
Penguin Books Canada Ltd, 2801 John Street,
Markham, Ontario, Canada L3R 1B4
Penguin Books (NZ) Ltd, 182–190 Wairau Road,
Auckland 10, New Zealand

Penguin Books Ltd, Registered Offices: Harmonds-
worth, Middlesex, England

First published in Great Britain by Hamish Hamilton Ltd 1991

10 9 8 7 6 5 4 3 2 1

Copyright © Dave Richards, 1991

The moral right of the author has been asserted

Filmset in 10 point Linotron Sabon by
Wyvern Typesetting Ltd, Bristol

Printed in Singapore by Toppan Printing Co., Ltd

A CIP catalogue record for this book is available
from the British Library

ISBN 0-241-12867-6

Contents

I realize that if I had to choose, I would rather have birds than airplanes.
                                                    Charles Lindbergh

*There is a way of life, a way of thinking, of behaving towards other men
and your fellow creatures, towards all living things, towards the whole earth
and the sky and the sun that is based on love, on compassion, on respect, on
cherishing everything there is around you because it is wonderful, unique,
it's natural and good and it evolved that way by itself, it's got to be
cherished and if we think like that and live that kind of life, we can all have
our freedom, we can all have our happiness, we can all feel the sun and
smell the grass and smell the flowers and look upon each other with
appreciation.*

                        John Gordon Davis: *Fear No Evil*

Introduction

Over one thousand species of bird – 1,065, to be precise – have been recorded in Kenya, making it one of the richest bird populations in Africa, if not the world. In Africa, only Zaïre boasts more species, and although there are countries in other parts of the world with larger bird counts, they tend also to have large regions of tropical forests, where birds are notoriously difficult to see. I would therefore go so far as to say that there is nowhere to match Kenya for general accessibility to good birding – and with its wonderful national park and national reserve system, a good network of roads, first-class and often luxurious accommodation, magnificent and varied scenery, perfect climate and friendly people, Kenya just can't be beaten as a tourist attraction. The animals and birds in the parks and reserves allow people to approach much closer than you might expect, because they are accustomed to the large numbers of tourists who regularly visit these areas.

One of the things I enjoy most on safari is sharing with clients or guests all the wonders that Kenya has to offer, and I hope that this book will encourage even more people to come here and enjoy them. However, for those who must remain armchair enthusiasts, I hope to share with you within the pages of this book a little of the glory of Kenya's birdlife.

I am often asked, 'Why birds?' I suppose, being brought up in England where there is relatively little animal wildlife, it is not surprising that birds became my main interest. As I learned more about them, I became intrigued by the fact that so many birds mysteriously disappeared every year when winter set in, only to reappear again in spring.

For many years Sunday was the highlight of the week. After Sunday school I would take a bus out of town and walk the country lanes, looking at the birdlife. I was fascinated by nature in general, and watched every nature programme I could on television. I particularly remember being spellbound by Armand and Michaela Denis's series, little knowing that years later I would live in a house only a hundred yards from their home, where much of their filming had been done.

For as long as I can recall I always wanted to own a camera, and I still remember saving up my pocket money and buying my first, an Ilford Sportsman, from the village post office. My next significant camera, bought in 1963, was a Russian Zenith, which gave me my first experience with interchangeable lenses; and I still remember how disappointed I was when the results with my first 'big lens', a 135 mm, didn't come up to my expectations. It was at this time that I met my wife Val's late uncle, Rowly Moore, a real camera buff; Rowly gave me much invaluable help, advice and, most important, lots of encouragement. It was the Zenith that I took to Africa.

I had wanted to visit Africa for a long time, but being newly married I had found the cost prohibitive. So when I spotted an advertisement for an aircraft maintenance engineer (which is what I was in those days) with the Zambia Flying Doctor Service (ZFDS), I saw too the chance to follow those birds that disappeared every year, and in October 1970 we found ourselves – much to Val's surprise, I might add – in Ndola, Zambia. The first birds that I recognized as I stepped off the plane were Eurasian House Martins. When we had left our house in England twelve hours earlier, there had still been a few House Martins feeding their young in nests under the eaves.

Two events stand out from the first couple of weeks in our new home. We met S. G. Madge, MBE – Graham – an English schoolteacher whose knowledge of, and enthusiasm for, birds were quite outstanding. Over the next two years I was to learn an extraordinary amount from him. And we visited our first national park. We flew with colleagues from the ZFDS to Luangwa National Park, at that time one of Africa's finest. Several things made lasting impressions on me that day. I was enthralled by the number and variety of birds and thrilled by our first sight of wild lions, but it was our first elephant that really impressed me: since that moment it has been my favourite animal. I was also deeply envious of our guide, wearing khaki shirt and shorts, safari boots (and no socks), driving an open Land Rover – and living in such a wonderful place. Little did I know that one day I would enjoy the same life-style.

It was while we were living in Ndola that I met George Reekie, another schoolteacher, and through him joined the Ndola Photographic Society, where I learned to take photographs. It was also about this time that I bought my first Canon camera, an FtQL; I am using Canon cameras to this day.

We spent three and a half very happy years in Zambia before moving to Nairobi, Kenya, where I took a position with a local aircraft maintenance company and then with an aerial survey company. In the course of this second job and in any spare time, I explored Kenya and travelled all over Africa, with extended periods in Tanzania and in Guinea, in West Africa. I joined the Nairobi Photographic Society and the East Africa Natural History Society (EANHS), and soon afterwards became one of the founder members of Scopus, the ornithological sub-committee of the EANHS, and also a member of the latter's Executive Committee.

1983 was a memorable year in the history of my photographic progress. In April I was awarded an Associateship of the Royal Photo-graphic Society of Great Britain and the following October a panel of slides earned me a Fellowship of the same society. The theme for both these distinctions was, of course, birds.

In 1984 I entered the safari business full-time, joining Ker and Downey Safaris Ltd, Nairobi, the oldest safari company in Africa. We specialize in luxury camping safaris, which generally means that we get away into some of the more remote areas of national parks and reserves. Camping in comfort is the best way to experience Africa, its sights, sounds and smells! Our camp food is legendary and numerous staff cater for every need.

Over the years I have, of course, built up quite a selection of nature slides, some of which have appeared in calendars, cards, magazines and books in Kenya and elsewhere. For some time I had nursed a vague ambition to write a book, illustrated entirely by my own photographs, and one day in late 1986 I was having lunch with Jonathan Scott, naturalist, photographer and author of *The Leopard's Tale*, amongst other books, when he suggested that I write to Caroline Taggart at Elm Tree Books/Hamish Hamilton and put my ideas to her. Well, many years later, here it is!

I have chosen to subdivide the book into national parks and reserves because it is there that most tourists will see birds, particularly around the game lodges. Out on a game drive few will fail to see a beautiful Lilac-breasted Roller, or an elegant Secretary Bird striding over the plains. Almost anyone who witnesses vultures feeding on a fresh kill will feel revulsion, but I hope when you have read a little about their lifestyle you will feel a little better disposed towards them.

There are many more ornithologically interesting places in Kenya, but most of these are for the really dedicated bird enthusiast. I have included two of these: Kenya's north coast (Chapter 11), an area visited by many tourists and, I must admit, a favourite of mine; and Lake Magadi (Chapter 12), a piece of wild Africa only seventy miles south of Nairobi.

It is not, and was never intended to be, another definitive 'guide book'. It is a selection of my favourite bird photographs, in which are included both some of the more common birds that the average tourist on a game-viewing safari in Kenya is likely to see, and a few rarer species to whet the appetite of the more experienced 'birder'. Classifying the birds was quite a task: because I have put a certain species under a certain national park or reserve, it doesn't mean it only occurs there, it simply means that that is where the photograph was taken. Very often – and the Lilac-breasted Roller is a good example – the bird is to be found in a number of other areas too. In the text I note whether it is widespread, confined to one area, or more likely to be found in a certain type of habitat. At the end of the introduction to each chapter I have listed other birds, illustrated elsewhere in the book, that you are likely to see in that particular region.

Whether you come on one of our luxury safaris, or stay in one of the beautiful game lodges, I promise you Kenya will exceed all your expectations.

I would like to take this opportunity to thank the government of Kenya for allowing me to live and work in their beautiful country.

To all visitors: *karibu* – welcome.

About the photographs

Almost every photograph in this book was taken from a vehicle, usually when I was on safari with clients. Some clients will, I'm sure, recognize some of the photographs, and probably have similar ones themselves.

I use Canon cameras and lenses; they are one of the few makes that can take all that Africa has to throw at them, day in, day out, year in, year out, and still work perfectly. I have several Canon A1 and T90 bodies, and the following lenses: 28–85 mm, f4; 100–300 mm, 4.5L; 400 mm, 4.5 and a 1.4X extender. I have recently acquired a 500 mm, 4.5L lens.

At one time it was *de rigueur* to show a highlight in a bird's eye (this made the bird in the photograph look really alive): now lenses have improved so much that even detail in a bird's eye can be seen.

I use Kodachrome 64, for me the only film for my type of photography and the only one that gives true colour reproduction. On occasions I have used Kodachrome 200, but I prefer K64 whenever possible. All my Kodachrome is sent to Switzerland for processing and I can't thank Kodak, Lausanne, enough for their excellent and prompt work over the years. I have not given the relevant speed and aperture for each photograph, but all were taken at between 1/250 and 1/500 of a second at f4.5–f8.

About the bird names

The English and scientific nomenclature used is from *Birds of East Africa*, edited by P. L. Britton, except in the case of the Short-toed Eagle, *Circaetus gallicus*. In this case I have used the common name: Black-chested Snake Eagle, an old term which in my opinion is much more suitable. If a bird is known by a more common name, I have included this in brackets after the English name. White-faced Whistling Duck (White-faced Tree Duck), *Dendrocygna viduata*, is a good example.

Acknowledgements

First of all I wish to thank my wife, Val, not only for typing all the original manuscript, but for her continued enthusiasm and help, without which this book would certainly have remained but a dream.

My sincere thanks also go to Graeme Backhurst for his comments on the manuscript; to Jonathan Scott for his generous help and encouragement over the years; and to Caroline Taggart (formerly of Elm Tree Books) for her continual advice and support, particularly during some of the difficult times, and latterly for her help in editing the text.

Over the years there have been many other people who have also given inspiration, help and advice, and to whom I express my gratitude: before Zambia, the late Rowly Moore; in Zambia, Graham Madge and George Reekie, members of the Zambia Ornithological Society's local group and of the Ndola Photographic Society; in Kenya, Jack and Pat Barrah, Reg and Ann Sampson, and Sol and Ruth Rabb earn special mention for their continuing strong support ever since our arrival. I would also like to thank all the members of Scopus, the Ornithological Subcommittee of the East Africa Natural History Society, and members of the Nairobi Photographic Society; and last, but not least, friends and colleagues at Ker and Downey Safaris and in the safari business in East Africa.

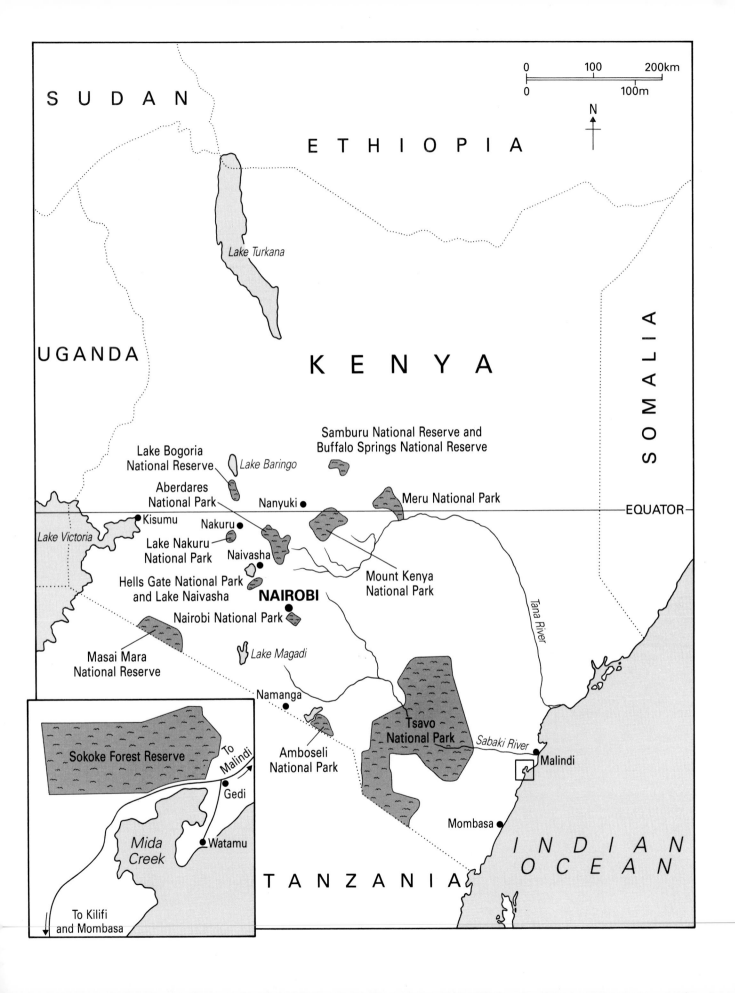

The Aberdares and Mount Kenya National Parks

The Aberdares National Park, north of Nairobi, consists of the Aberdares mountain range, running north–south, and a forested salient extending down the eastern slopes. The park consists mainly of magnificent, gently rolling moorland at an altitude of 10,000 feet, with large areas of giant heath, forest patches of rosewood, St John's wort and bamboo species. There are many boggy areas, small pools and cold streams flowing across the moorland; there are also several spectacular waterfalls. As you descend into the salient, you pass through a zone of hagenia and bamboo, which slowly gives way to mountain forest as it drops to about 6,500 feet. I am by no means alone in considering this the most beautiful part of the park. It is here that the world-famous lodges Treetops (where Princess Elizabeth was staying when she became Queen on the death of her father in 1952) and the Ark are to be found. Because of the severity of the terrain, everyone except visitors to the two lodges, or professional safari companies equipped with strong four-wheel-drive vehicles, has to obtain permission from the warden before entering the salient.

Mount Kenya National Park comprises all the area around the mountain above the 3,200 metre (about 10,000 feet) contour. Mount Kenya is now a little over 17,000 feet, but at one time it was much higher: after centuries of erosion only the hard volcanic central plug is left. With a four-wheel-drive vehicle it is possible to drive to just below 10,000 feet. As in the Aberdares, the lower slopes are forest-covered, with the giant Pencil Cedar (*Juniperus procera*) and Podo (*Podocarpus sp.*) trees very prominent. These slowly give way to the hagenia/bamboo zone and hypericum (St John's wort), which in turn give way to moorland and glaciers. At Mountain Lodge, the game-viewing lodge on Mount Kenya, it is possible to see the rarely recorded Mackinder's Eagle Owl, named after the first European to climb the mountain.

Birdlife in these two parks can be very varied and abundant, particularly on a bright sunny morning. The most magnificent resident is the Crowned Eagle, which can usually be seen soaring high above the forest; a pair with young in the salient of the Aberdares recently starred in the BBC film of the Great Rift Valley. There are many sunbirds to be seen, perhaps the most conspicuous being the Golden-winged Sunbird, usually observed feeding on crotolaria flowers, known locally as Lion's Claw because of the shape of the blooms. Driving along a forest track you can be confident of seeing a flash of bright crimson as a Hartlaub's Turaco swoops overhead.

In addition to those birds featured below, you might also see the Speckled Mousebird, Dusky Flycatcher and Northern Olive Thrush.

Red-eyed Dove

Streptopelia semitorquata

Although it is found throughout Kenya, except in the very dry low country, the Red-eyed Dove is particularly common in the Highlands. Its distinctive 'coo, coo, cook-coo-cuk-coo' call is a feature of a visit to this area.

It is often confused with the Mourning Dove, but can be distinguished by its conspicuous pale forehead and red eye-ring with surrounding red skin.

Long-tailed Widowbird

Euplectes progne

The male of this species is very striking, and you are most likely to see him when travelling to or between the Aberdares and Mount Kenya National Parks. His laboured display-flight is a common sight near marshy areas in the open grasslands.

Once the breeding season is over the male moults, shedding his long tail-feathers and slowly turning into an inconspicuous little brown bird like the female. The male is polygamous, leaving the female with sole responsibility for nest-building, incubation and rearing of chicks.

Crowned Eagle

Stephanoaetus coronatus

To my mind this is the finest of all the African eagles, and although it is not the largest it is the most powerful, regularly taking prey up to five times its own weight. There are reports of Crowned Eagles attacking domestic stock, and even cats and dogs. Once, when I was living in Zambia, I heard of an immature Crowned Eagle attacking and seriously injuring a seven-year-old boy before being beaten off and killed by an African woman using a hoe.

The Crowned Eagle usually hunts in the early morning or late evening, waiting patiently on a perch over a game trail or an open forest glade. Its large, powerful talons are capable of killing prey as large as an immature bushbuck, but it more regularly preys on the suni (the tiny forest antelope), or on monkeys, hyraxes and squirrels.

I have seen a Crowned Eagle with prey on a few memorable occasions. Once, in Nairobi National Park, I came across two Tawny Eagles harassing a Crowned Eagle which was perched in a tree with an adult Sykes monkey hanging from one of its claws. The Crowned Eagle's talons were firmly grasping the monkey's head, and it had great difficulty flying away with its prey to escape the Tawny Eagles. It succeeded in the end, but the Tawnies did not give up the chase for some time. (This is typical 'pirate' behaviour for a Tawny Eagle.)

On another evening I found a Crowned Eagle in the Aberdares National Park, sitting in a tree about ten feet off the ground. Its crop was bulging with food and in its talons it held what appeared to be the remains of the shoulder and leg of an immature bushbuck. As I watched, a leopard came out of the dense vegetation carrying the rest of the carcass, which it had presumably scavenged from the eagle.

In a further incident, again in the Aberdares, I saw a Crowned Eagle dive out of a high tree and disappear into the undergrowth some way ahead. When I arrived at the spot I found the eagle holding down a suni.

If the eagle kills its prey on the ground and the prey is too heavy to lift, it will be dragged into the undergrowth, where it will be dismembered and the various parts cached in trees out of reach of other predators.

The Crowned Eagle can be found in thick riverine woodlands and small forest patches, but its preferred habitat is the forest of the Aberdares and Mount Kenya National Parks in Kenya.

It usually perches well hidden inside a tall tree and is therefore easy to miss, but it can sometimes be seen high on a prominent, exposed perch. You are most likely to see – and hear – it during its impressive display-flight, when it exhibits its distinctive chestnut underwing coverts and the bold barring on its very rounded wings and long tail.

During this display-flight the male soars high over his territory before beginning a series of swooping dives and spectacular climbs, in the course of which he calls continuously. Sometimes this display takes place so high in the sky – several thousand feet above the forest – that the birds are invisible to the human eye, but even then the call can usually be heard quite clearly. While I write I can hear a Crowned Eagle calling over the Ololua Forest at Karen, near Nairobi, where I live.

At the end of the display the male often dives towards the female, who turns on her back presenting her talons, before they disappear into the forest canopy.

Golden-winged Sunbird

Nectarinia reichenowi

A common Highland bird with a prominent, long, decurved bill, the Golden-winged Sunbird occurs along forest glades where it feeds on the crotolaria and leonotis flowers. Like the Malachite Sunbird, it descends to lower altitudes in cool, wet weather.

Augur Buzzard

Buteo augur

A common resident of the Highlands, the Augur Buzzard is also found at lower altitudes where there are rocky outcrops and steep-sided hills, such as in Tsavo National Park. You are most likely to see it soaring high in the sky (its conspicuous red tail is a wonderful sight), but it also spends a lot of time sitting on exposed branches and even on telegraph-poles and fence posts along the roadside. Its strident 'aung-aung-aung' call is unmistakable.

The Augur Buzzard feeds on small mammals such as rats and mice, and in the high moorlands captures huge mole rats, which may be as much as a third of its own size.

Robin Chat

Cossypha caffra

The Robin Chat is a common resident of the Highland forests, usually found in pairs at forest edges or along the many tracks. It is quite tame, and becomes even tamer near human habitation. It is usually seen hopping along the ground, bobbing and flirting its tail as it searches for food. The Robin Chat has an appealing habit of jerking its tail upwards and fanning it, especially after landing or when alarmed.

Robins are a link with colonial times: wherever the British settled they tended to find a bird with a red breast and call it a robin, to remind them of home and the original Robin Redbreast so often depicted on Christmas cards. The East African Robin Chat is in fact a member of the thrush family (as is the American Robin, while the Australian Robin is really a flycatcher).

The Robin Chat's nest is often parasitized by the Red-chested Cuckoo.

7

Jackson's Francolin

Francolinus jacksoni

This shy but handsome francolin is found in both the Aberdares and Mount Kenya National Parks and is endemic to Kenya. It appears to be more common at higher altitudes, either in the bamboo forest or among the large tussocks of grass on the moorlands where this picture was taken.

Its call is high-pitched and extremely loud in the early morning and evening; it also emits a low chuckling call when feeding, possibly to enable it to keep in contact with others of its kind in the dense undergrowth.

Alpine Chat

Cercomela sordida

The Alpine Chat, also known as the Hill or Mountain Chat, is a drab-looking little bird, but it is both tame and friendly.

It is common on the moorlands and its conspicuous white tail-feathers usually reveal its presence as it flies from perch to perch. Anyone visiting or picnicking by one of the waterfalls in the Aberdares National Park, or staying at one of the climbers' huts on Mount Kenya, will soon find these chats approaching to scrounge for titbits.

Cinnamon-chested Bee-eater

Merops oreobates

This large bee-eater is often seen swooping after prey, before returning to a perch where it sits, usually with others, slowly wagging its tail backwards and forwards. It can also be seen flying out of its nest-hole in the embankments along the national park tracks.

As it tends to be cold at night in these Highland areas, Cinnamon-chested Bee-eaters often roost in groups, presumably to keep warm. One evening I watched a number of them gathering together along a branch: as each new bird arrived it would land in the middle of the group, often on the back of another bird, and force its way down on to the branch. Occasionally, one of the birds that had been edged to the outside of the group would fly up and push back into the centre. This went on until there were about nine birds in the group and the dark and rain made it impossible for me to watch any longer.

Hartlaub's Turaco

Tauraco hartlaubi

Although this bird is quite common in the Highland parks, all that most visitors see of it is a brilliant flash of red as it swoops from tree to tree. Even when the turaco is perching it can be difficult to have a clear sight of it as within moments it quickly bounces and runs through the branches, disappearing from view and leaving behind just the sound of its harsh, high-pitched, 'kaw-kaw' call.

It sometimes feeds on caterpillars and insects, but seems to prefer fruit in season, in particular the berry of *Carissa edulis*. The young in the photo were fed almost exclusively on this fruit while I was observing them.

All turacos are extremely agile and able to move quickly and silently along branches with a light, springy action. This is because of a unique adaptation of their feet: the outer toe is at right angles to the foot and is free to move backwards and forwards.

Another unique feature of the turacos is the pigmentation of their feathers. Most birds owe their colouring to the refraction of light through the hollow shafts of their feathers. Turaco feathers contain a red and a green pigment, both unique to the Turaco family. The red pigment contains copper and, extraordinarily enough, appears to be soluble in water.

11

White-starred Forest Robin

Pogonocichla stellata

A relative of the European robin, the White-starred Forest Robin is common in the Highland forests but, in spite of its brilliant chest colouring, is very inconspicuous – the plumage on its back is very drab, and if it turns its back on you it seems almost to disappear. Because of this effective camouflage it can be elusive, but once found it is often quite tame.

It gets its name from a black-edged, brilliant white spot at the base of its throat which is normally visible only during display. At this time two more white spots, one above each eye, appear to expand, giving the impression of two headlights shining in the poor forest light.

Perhaps the best way to locate this bird is by listening first for its song, a strange, almost mournful, flute-like whistle.

Amboseli National Park

This is Hemingway country, and although Amboseli is famous for its big game – and snow-capped Kilimanjaro, at 19,340 feet Africa's highest mountain, forming a superb backdrop – it is also one of the best areas of Kenya for seeing and photographing a large variety of wonderful birds. This is partly due to its varied landscape of dry lake-beds, open plains, acacia woodland, thornbush, and several large swamps, but also because most of the resident birds are quite used to the sight of tourist vehicles and pay little attention to them, allowing anyone who is interested in birds to approach quite closely.

On the open plains look out for the stately Kori Bustard, Two-banded Courser, Crowned Plover, Sandgrouse and various larks and pipits. In the forest and thornbush, you should see the Martial Eagle, Pale Chanting Goshawk, Lilac-breasted Roller, Von der Decken's Hornbill, woodpeckers and the beautiful Taveta Golden Weaver. Even more rewarding are the lakes and swamps, Amboseli's real draw for the bird-watcher. It is not uncommon on a morning's game-drive to see ten species of heron! And nowhere else is the lovely Malachite Kingfisher so numerous or so tame.

Although the film *Where No Vultures Fly*, starring Anthony Steele and Dinah Sheridan, was made in Amboseli, I have recorded there seven different species of vulture, including the rare Palm-nut Vulture.

In addition to the birds featured in this chapter or mentioned above, you might see Ostrich, Purple Heron, Great White Egret, Yellow-billed Egret, Little Egret, Saddle-billed Stork, Yellow-billed Stork, African Spoonbill, Pygmy Goose, White-backed Vulture, Lappet-faced Vulture, Pygmy Falcon, Martial Eagle, Bateleur, African Fish Eagle, Pale Chanting Goshawk, Black Crake, Crowned Crane, Kori Bustard, Water Thicknee, Kittlitz's Sandplover, Crowned Plover, Two-banded Courser, Namaqua Dove, White-browed Coucal, Eurasian Roller, Lilac-breasted Roller, Pied Kingfisher, Red-billed Hornbill, Verreaux's Eagle Owl, Superb Starling and Grosbeak Weaver.

Pink-backed Pelican

Pelecanus rufescens

Although less numerous than the White Pelican, the Pink-backed is far more widespread and can be found on almost any water where there may be fish – even on small dams, coastal lagoons and sewage and settling ponds.

It normally occurs singly or in small groups, but during roosting and nesting it is very gregarious. The Pink-backed Pelican both roosts and nests in trees, in marked contrast to the White Pelican which roosts and nests on the ground. I never cease to be amazed that the Pink-backed should choose to spend its time in trees, as it looks most ungainly moving about on thin, spindly branches.

The Pink-backed Pelican usually fishes alone, slowly gliding through the water with head and neck pulled back and head held at an angle. On sighting its prey it plunges its head forward with great speed and, if successful, lifts its bill slowly to drain out the water before tipping its head back and swallowing the fish.

Although predominantly light grey in colour, this pelican takes its name from the soft pink plumage of the adult's back, usually visible when it is preening.

15

Grey Heron

Ardea cinerea

A shy, solitary bird, the Grey Heron is usually observed standing motionless in the shallows or on the banks of rivers or lakes, with its neck stretched out as it peers down into the water.

It feeds mostly in the early morning or late afternoon, but also at night if there is moonlight; its diet consists of fish, frogs and aquatic insects. Its eyes, like those of other herons, are set well forward in the head, providing good binocular vision when it stabs its prey.

The bird in the photograph was not as shy as these herons are normally. It was standing in a small pool on the edge of Enkongo Narok Swamp in Amboseli and twenty yards away a pride of lions was feeding on a zebra. The pride was surrounded by a number of tourist vehicles, all of the occupants engrossed in photographing the lions. Several people looked at me in disbelief as I ignored the kill and photographed the heron instead!

Egyptian Vulture

Neophron percnopterus

Of all the vulture family the Egyptian Vulture is most closely associated with man. In ancient Egypt it was called Pharaoh's Chicken, and up to a hundred years or so ago it was common in Cairo, acting as the city's sanitation system.

Nowadays it is usually found in Masai country, feeding on offal, refuse and even human excrement. It is often seen on kills in the national parks; but, probably because it is smaller than most other vultures, it seems to be the lowest in the pecking order, only picking up small scraps left by other birds or tearing at whatever pieces of flesh might still cling to the bones. It will also feed on scraps left around hyena and wild dog dens. Although primarily a scavenger, the Egyptian Vulture has been known to kill young flamingo and ostrich chicks.

The Egyptian Vulture is well known for its liking for eggs – unusual food for a vulture. It has been recorded picking up flamingo and pelican eggs and dashing them to the ground to break them open. Ostrich eggs are too large for it to lift, so the vulture picks up stones and small rocks, which may be as much as two pounds in weight. It then repeatedly throws the stones down on to the egg until it breaks. This is one of the very few known instances of a bird using a tool.

In its immature plumage this vulture can easily be confused with the Hooded Vulture, but in adulthood, although it bears a slight resemblance to the Palm-nut Vulture, the strongly contrasting black and white wings, clearly visible in flight, and the long, white, wedge-shaped tail are unmistakable.

17

Cattle Egret

Bubulcus ibis

This normally white bird was originally known as the Buff-backed Heron: not a very appropriate name as its buff colouring appears only during the breeding season. Also inaccurately called the Tick Bird, the Cattle Egret feeds mainly on insects disturbed by grazing animals. It is often seen perched on large mammals and will undoubtedly take ticks if available.

The Cattle Egret is gregarious and prefers to live not too far from water, where the African buffalo is its favoured host companion. After the rains, it often accompanies herds of buffalo, usually flying alongside and picking up insects disturbed by them. If the grass is very long, the presence of the Cattle Egret may be the only indication of the buffaloes' approach.

It has also been known to travel long distances from water and can be found feeding alongside zebra and other plains game. In the evening you may see a group of Cattle Egrets flying low in V-formation as they return to roost, usually in trees or tall reeds near a lake or swamp.

The Cattle Egret has become much more common during the last fifty years as more and more of the African bush is cleared for cattle ranching, creating an ideal habitat. It has even spread as far afield as Australia and New Zealand and can be found in most states of the USA.

Long-toed Plover

Vanellus crassirostris

This bird is quite common in the Lake Victoria basin, but generally uncommon elsewhere. It occurs singly or in small family groups in marshland, swamps and freshwater pools where there is floating vegetation to house the insects on which it feeds. It has also been seen in flooded grassland and even rice paddies.

The Long-toed Plover (*left*) is able to walk on the floating pads of water-lilies, like the Jacana. Normally rather shy, when breeding it becomes very aggressive and has been known to attack birds as large as the Goliath Heron.

In Amboseli the best place to see the Long-toed Plover is the Enkongo Narok Swamp, near the Causeway, where this photo was taken.

Black-winged Stilt

Himantopus himantopus

With the exception of the flamingoes, the Black-winged Stilt (*right*) has the longest legs in proportion to its body size of any water bird. Its long legs allow it to feed in deeper water than can most other waders; it mainly takes aquatic insects from the surface of the water, but also feeds on tadpoles and small fish.

It is a distinctive black-and-white bird with red legs, more usually seen in the alkaline lakes of the Rift Valley, but it also occurs – and breeds – on the edges of the Enkongo Narok Swamp in Amboseli.

Tawny Eagle

Aquila rapax

The Tawny Eagle is a common resident with variable plumage, ranging in colour from very pale to dark brown. This variation often makes it difficult to identify, and even if the adult bird is of the most usual colour – dark tawny brown – it may be confused with the Brown Snake Eagle, Wahlberg's Eagle, its near relative the migrant Steppe Eagle, and other brown eagles.

The Tawny has been much reviled as a scavenger. It is most often seen feeding on the remains of a dead animal, frequently with vultures on a lion kill. It also steals food from other birds of prey, including even the mighty Marabou Stork, making it a pirate and adding to its already tarnished reputation.

It is, nevertheless, a capable hunter in its own right, swooping down on to its prey from a high perch or from the air. It will kill small mammals such as dik-diks, hares and young gazelles; it will also feed on game birds and is well known for raiding the breeding colonies of Quelea. It has been recorded killing small bustards, young ostriches and flamingoes and at times, when termites are swarming or grasshoppers or locusts are common, it will even feed on these highly nutritious creatures.

Painted Snipe

Rostratula benghalensis

Although there is a resemblance in appearance this is not a true snipe, differing as it does from other members of the family in a number of ways, and claiming in fact a closer relationship to the Jacana. It is generally uncommon and easy to overlook because of its shy, skulking habits. Feeding mainly at twilight on exposed mud on the edge of lakes, swamps and rivers, it always stays close to cover so that it can hide quickly. When disturbed it usually freezes, making it even more difficult to see.

The Painted Snipe is unusual in several respects. The female is larger and much more brightly coloured than the male and is poly-androus, laying several clutches of eggs, each for a different male. She pairs with at least two, often as many as four, males. The male is thought to be responsible for building the nest, and after the female has laid her eggs, usually four at a time, the pair bond is broken and she leaves the incubation and rearing of the young to the male. Although the female takes no part in the rearing of the young she stays in the area, perhaps to defend her territory.

There are two other species of bird which are known to have similar behaviour patterns. The Phalaropes and Sanderling both breed in the Arctic, where the breeding season is very short, so polyandry is most likely a way of producing more young in the limited time available – but this hardly explains why the Painted Snipe evolved this way.

Malachite Kingfisher

Alcedo cristata

This small (five inches long) and brilliantly coloured bird is surely the most beautiful of all the African kingfishers. It gets its name from the malachite colour of its crest.

It is quite common, occurring by all freshwater lakes, rivers and streams, and is usually seen waiting quietly, occasionally bobbing its head as it sits on a reed stem or branch overlooking the water. It feeds on small fish and tadpoles, and catches them by diving, beak first, into the water. It then returns to its perch, where it will beat its prey several times before swallowing it head first.

In flight the Malachite Kingfisher is a gorgeous sight as it darts swiftly over the surface of the water. Like others of its kind it nests in burrows, which it excavates in a vertical bank, usually by a river.

Pygmy Kingfisher

Ispidina picta

The Pygmy Kingfisher is similar to, although a little smaller than, the Malachite Kingfisher, the main difference being the absence of the distinctive malachite crest.

The Pygmy Kingfisher is primarily a bird of forest, woodland and bush country, but is also often found near water. In either case it feeds on insects. It is usually seen sitting motionless, apart from the occasional bobbing of the head, in the shade of a bush, from which it will dive down when it sights its prey.

Like the Malachite Kingfisher it nests in burrows in vertical banks.

Squacco Heron

Ardeola ralloides

At times the Squacco Heron is a common resident of the Amboseli swamps. Usually solitary, it is most often found among the reed-beds where, because of its cryptic colouring, it is inconspicuous. If disturbed it quickly flies away, revealing white wings, rump and tail – and suddenly we spy a 'new' bird. But when it lands all the white disappears as it takes up its normal hunched stance.

It catches its prey – insects, beetles, frogs and small fish – by stalking slowly through shallow water.

The photograph shows the Squacco Heron in its breeding plumage; in its non-breeding plumage it looks similar to a less frequent visitor to Amboseli, the Madagascar Squacco Heron.

Goliath Heron

Ardea goliath

Standing five feet tall, this is the world's largest heron. It is usually found in freshwater lakes and swamps, the Enkongo Narok Swamp in Amboseli being a particularly popular habitat. It is normally solitary.

When hunting, the Goliath either walks slowly through shallow water or stands motionless waiting for fish to swim by. It holds its head horizontally to catch large fish such as tilapia and catfish, which it stabs with its bill. Then it drops its prey among the reed-beds, and quickly snatches it up again to swallow it head first. After swallowing a fish it will usually take a drink of water.

Herons like to sunbathe. This Goliath Heron had been sitting hunched up on a dull morning. When eventually the sun came out he opened up his wings, and then folded them into a heraldic position to enjoy the warmth.

The Goliath Heron is similar in appearance to the much smaller Purple Heron, but remembering the size difference and the more retiring behaviour of the Purple Heron should put an end to any confusion.

African Marsh Harrier

Circus ranivorus

The African Marsh Harrier is a very localized and uncommon resident of swamps and marshes. It can be observed hunting over grasslands, but it has a definite preference for the swamps, where it also breeds. Its numbers have declined in recent years, probably because of the continuing drainage of the wetlands for agricultural purposes. Even so, it is often absent from some apparently suitable habitats. Perhaps the fact that Kenya is the most northerly part of its range may be the explanation.

It hunts by flying low over the reeds or grass (often in the same areas as those frequented by Marsh Owls at night). Its flight is slow and laboured. When it spots prey, it is able to stop immediately, before plunging with long legs and talons extended. Sometimes, in a spectacular acrobatic display, it will perform a half-roll and a backward turn in pursuit of its prey.

The Marsh Harrier feeds on a variety of small creatures, mainly rats, mice, young birds, frogs and insects. But it has also been recorded snatching fish from just below the water's surface, catching wounded birds shot by hunters, killing birds as large as the Red-billed Teal, and raiding heronries for eggs and young.

It nests low down in a swamp or marsh and has been recorded nesting as little as ten feet from a Marsh Owl. The female does most of the incubating, and during this time she is frequently fed by the male, who drops food for her. Occasionally the female will fly up, roll on to her back with her legs outstretched, and receive food directly from her mate. She keeps the nest site meticulously clean, always disposing of any uneaten food items.

Lake Bogoria National Reserve and Lake Baringo

Lake Bogoria used to be called Lake Hannington after Bishop Hannington, who 'discovered' it in 1885 on his way to Uganda, where he was murdered. Until recently this lake and the dramatic scenery that surrounds it were almost inaccessible: only adventurous types with strong 4WD vehicles dared venture down to it. Now all has changed and there is a tarmac road leading off the Nakuru-Baringo road, near Marigat, which takes you down to the lake and part way along the western shore, as far as the first major hot springs.

Although Lake Bogoria, with steam jets, geysers and fumaroles along its shore, is principally a scenic reserve – and arguably the most dramatic of all the Rift Valley lakes – at times it is home to hundreds of thousands of flamingoes which feed on Spirulina in its alkaline waters. There can be few more spectacular sights than these flamingoes gathering together in tight flocks to drink and bathe in the hot but fresh water running from the many geysers, against the dramatic backdrop of the eastern wall of the Great Rift Valley. Some years Lesser Flamingoes build nests, but there is little evidence of actual breeding taking place: they seem to prefer an even more remote and inaccessible Rift Valley lake, Lake Natron, just over the border in Tanzania.

The area surrounding the lake is inhospitable thornbush country, but it is a good place to see the Dark Chanting Goshawk, Black-headed Plover, Greater and Lesser Flamingoes, African Spoonbill, Tawny Eagle, Fish Eagle, Black-winged Stilt, Avocet and Rufous-crowned Roller, in addition to the birds detailed in this chapter.

Lake Baringo, by contrast, is a freshwater lake and a paradise for anyone interested in birds: over 400 species have been recorded there. A boat trip along the lake shore and up the Molo River, if it is flowing, is often the highlight of any safari: you can see and photograph from only a few feet away the magnificent Goliath Heron or dainty Jacana, to mention only two of the many birds that can be seen every day from the boat.

Almost immediately west of the lake is a sheer escarpment of volcanic rock, and an early morning walk along its base with the lodge's resident guide is unarguably the best bird walk in East Africa – indeed, perhaps anywhere in the world.

One of the escarpment's main attractions is a pair of Verreaux's Eagles which regularly nests there; on your walk you are also sure to see many uncommon birds such as Hemprich's Hornbill and the Bristle-crowned Starling. The remainder of the lake is surrounded by dry thornbush, but for the keen birder there is a wealth of birds to be found there.

Others you might see include the Pink-backed Pelican, Purple Heron, Kestrel, Fish Eagle and Yellow-billed Hornbill.

Red and Yellow Barbet
Trachyphonus erythrocephalus

This distinctive and strikingly coloured bird is quite common in dry bush country. Its loud, unmistakable, duetting call, particularly in the early morning, is a feature of the African bush and one of the many delightful sounds often heard by campers.

The sexes are similar in colour, except that the male has a black crown while the female's is red.

The Red and Yellow Barbet usually excavates a tunnel for its nest, but can also often be found nesting inside tall, chimney-like termite mounds. Its normal diet is termites and other insects, but it has been known to eat lizards.

Cape Wigeon
Anas capensis

This charming little duck with its unmistakable pale spotted plumage and pink bill is generally common on the alkaline lakes of the Rift Valley, where it feeds on aquatic insects, crustacea and vegetable matter. It is usually found in pairs or small groups.

White-faced Whistling Duck (White-faced Tree Duck)

Dendrocygna viduata

A common and highly gregarious species, this duck is usually found on freshwater lakes, marshes, flooded grasslands or at the coast. Its old name of tree duck arose because in India, where it also occurs, it apparently regularly roosts and nests in trees, something that it rarely does in East Africa. Its modern name is self-explanatory, and hearing its beautifully clear, three-syllable whistle as it flies overhead is one of the delights of walking in the African bush.

The White-faced Whistling Duck is most active in the early morning and late afternoon, flying to and from its feeding areas, where it eats grass, seeds and corms. It spends the rest of the day just sitting on a bank or in shallow water, preening itself, or very often in pairs with both birds preening each other.

Beautiful Sunbird

Nectarinia pulchella

Sunbirds, although not related to the humming-birds of the Americas, fill a similar ecological niche. Both feed on nectar and small insects taken from flowers but, whereas the humming-bird hovers expertly when feeding, the sunbird usually perches on the stems of flowers in order to eat. If it hovers it is only for a few seconds, and with nothing like the skill of the humming-bird. It has a very rapid and erratic flight as it darts from flower to flower.

Like humming-birds, sunbirds have very long, slender, curved bills and long, hollow tongues which enable them to feed deep inside a flower, though if they are unable to reach the nectar in a large flower they will pierce a hole at the base. As they feed, their heads are dusted with pollen, which they carry from flower to flower, fertilizing the plants in the process, and thus giving back something in return for the nectar.

Male sunbirds are usually more brightly coloured than the females, and the Beautiful Sunbird is a good example. The male is green with a bright red chest, while the female is a drab brown above with streaky brown underparts.

As its name suggests, this is a beautiful bird, common in the dry bush country of East Africa. There are two quite distinct subspecies: one, occurring to the east of the Rift Valley and in the drier areas near Lake Victoria, has a black belly; the other, found to the west of the Rift, is green-bellied.

The Beautiful Sunbird feeds on most flowers, but is particularly partial to flowering aloes and acacia blossoms.

Allen's Gallinule

Porphyrio alleni

An uncommon and shy bird, Allen's Gallinule can often be seen at Lake Baringo between June and September. Although it seems to prefer dense reed-beds and flooded grassland, it can sometimes be observed walking on waterlilies, like the Jacana. The visitor's best chance of seeing Allen's Gallinule is by taking a boat trip from one of the lodges at Lake Baringo, ideally in a boat that is able to navigate the Molo River.

Darter
(Snake Bird)
Anhinga rufa

The Darter differs in appearance from the very similar cormorant in that it has a much longer, slimmer neck and a sharp, pointed bill. It is usually seen perched on a bare branch over water, often with its wings stretched out to dry. When flying it moves low over the surface of the water, holding its neck steady but with its characteristic kink.

Water birds are able to stay buoyant by trapping air between their feathers. When a Darter wishes to dive for a fish or a frog it squeezes its feathers, forcing out the trapped air. When chasing prey through water it uses its wings – 'flying through the water', as it were – and often impales its prey on the end of its bill.

The Darter can also be detected swimming with its body submerged and only its head and neck above the water. In this posture it looks remarkably like a snake, and is often called the Snake Bird because of it.

Hemprich's Hornbill
Tockus hemprichii

This uncommon hornbill is one of the great attractions for visitors to Lake Baringo. Although it can be seen on Island Camp in the middle of the lake, it is more usual to spot it on the huge cliffs on the west side, where it nests in crevices.

Blue-cheeked Bee-eater

Merops persicus

This beautiful bird with its glorious colouring breeds in the Middle East and visits East Africa between October and April. It is found in small flocks, usually near water, and the Lake Baringo Club is a good place for visitors to see it: it often perches on the outermost branches of the trees nearest the lake shore.

The bee-eaters are my favourite family of birds. Not only are they lovely in appearance, but their swift, even aerobatic, flight in pursuit of prey is a wonder to behold. The Blue-cheeked Bee-eater feeds mainly on dragonflies and other flying insects found over water, but if honeybees are plentiful it will take them too. Like other bee-eaters, it beats and dismembers the bee before swallowing it.

When the Blue-cheeked Bee-eater departs from Baringo in mid-April, it is almost immediately replaced by the Madagascar Bee-eater, which even feeds from the same trees. This visitor stays in the Baringo area until September/October, when it heads for its breeding areas.

Hell's Gate National Park and Lake Naivasha

Although only recently created a national park, Hell's Gate has long been known as a nesting site of the very rare (in East Africa) Lammergeyer or Bearded Vulture. The sheer, dramatic cliffs, 400 feet high, are popular with rock climbers, and unfortunately this has caused some disturbance in the past. Also nesting on the cliffs are Rüppell's Vultures, along with large colonies of two different species of swift.

The area is known locally as Ol Njorowa, and the park entrance is dominated by a pinnacle of rock known as Fischer's Column, named after a Dr Fischer who was ambushed there by the Masai in 1882.

Other birds commonly seen here include the Secretary Bird, Egyptian Vulture, White-backed Vulture and White-fronted Bee-eater.

Lake Naivasha, at over 6,000 feet, is the highest of all the Rift Valley lakes, and I think it is the most beautiful. Unfortunately, over the years the ecological balance of the lake has been seriously disturbed by the introduction of various foreign plants, animals and aquatic life. Chief amongst them is the South American coypu, which ate all the spectacular beds of water-lilies that provided a home for numerous birds such as the Purple Gallinule and the Jacana. At the time of writing the water-lilies appear to be staging a comeback, so with a little luck the lake will recover some of its former glory. In spite of these problems Lake Naivasha is still a wonderful place to visit, and a must for the bird enthusiast.

The lake is fringed with papyrus — and with the extinct volcano Mount Longonot as a backdrop it is a marvellous place to watch birds, particularly on a boat trip from one of the lodges. In the boat you can closely approach cormorants with their wings stretched out to dry, Pink-backed Pelicans, herons and Fish Eagles. The land bordering the lake is mostly private farmland, but at the lodges there are still areas of acacia woodland which are rich in birdlife.

You may also see the Goliath Heron, Great White Egret, Saddle-billed Stork, Jacana, White-fronted Bee-eater, Paradise Flycatcher and Grey-backed Fiscal.

Rüppell's Vulture
(Rüppell's Griffon Vulture)

Gyps rueppellii

A generally common species, the Rüppell's Vulture is nevertheless rare in some parts of East Africa because of the absence of cliffs and gorges, on which it roosts and breeds. It differs from the similar White-backed Vulture mainly in having white edging to its body feathers, a pale bill and yellow eye. On a carcass the Rüppell's can dominate the White-backed, being slightly larger, heavier and more powerful. It has a long bare neck and, like the White-backed, can feed deep inside a carcass.

In common with the White-backed vulture it is unable to fly very far without the aid of hot air thermals, but it can usually leave its roost earlier, only an hour or two after sunrise, taking advantage of the height and stronger winds associated with the gorges and cliffs where it roosts.

Lammergeyer
(Bearded Vulture)

Gypaetus barbatus

A large and imposing vulture with a wing span of eight feet, the Lammergeyer occurs in mountains, cliffs and gorges. In flight it is magnificent, with a silhouette distinguished by long tapered wings and a diamond-shaped tail. The visitor is most likely to see it, singly or in pairs, soaring majestically in the sky: it prefers to fly very high and has been recorded at above 26,000 feet in the Himalayas.

It is fairly rare in East Africa but a pair used to breed at Hell's Gate near Lake Naivasha, and can sometimes still be seen there. Unfortunately the nest site was close to a route much favoured by rock climbers, and the Lammergeyers couldn't tolerate all the disturbance.

The Lammergeyer is well known for its habit of breaking bones by dropping them on to rocks, so that it can feed more easily on the bone marrow. It does this by flying downwind, holding the bone pointing forward to reduce air resistance; as it nears the dropping point it dives sharply to increase speed, then releases the bone. This

means that the bird can choose a suitable point for the bone to hit, and judge accurately where it will fall from a height of well over a hundred feet. The Lammergeyer then descends rapidly, turning into the wind as it lands, only moments after the bone. If the bone has failed to break, the Lammergeyer simply repeats the process.

The Lammergeyer's tongue is specially adapted so that it can extract bone marrow, but it will also eat little pieces of bone.

This is the bird that is reputed to drop tortoises on to rocks so that it can eat the flesh; according to Pliny, the Greek dramatist Aeschylus was killed when a Lammergeyer dropped a tortoise on him, apparently mistaking his bald head for a rock.

41

Pied Kingfisher

Ceryle rudis

A characteristic bird of Lake Naivasha, the Pied Kingfisher is also common on most lakes and rivers, and at the coast. It is noisy and tame and usually seen in pairs or small groups.

The Pied Kingfisher uses a convenient perch to look out for prey, and when perched will repeatedly raise and lower its tail. It has a very conspicuous habit of hovering over the water before diving in, head first, to capture its prey, and this graceful movement is always a delight to watch. It will then carry its prey back to a favourite perch and beat it soundly before eating it, head first.

This is an easy bird to sex, the male having two black bands, one thick and one thin, across his chest, while the female has only one band, which is broken in the middle.

Greater Cormorant (White-breasted Cormorant)

Phalacrocorax carbo

A gregarious bird common on most of East Africa's lakes, both alkaline and fresh, the Greater Cormorant is usually to be discovered sitting along the shore or on rocks or bare branches – and even on the backs of sleeping hippos – in its characteristic pose, with wings outstretched. One reason for this posture is that cormorants'

feathers are less water-repellent than those of other water birds; they very quickly become waterlogged and need to be dried out after fishing. The pose is also thought to aid digestion and to help the bird regulate its temperature.

This feature of feather-waterlogging may help cormorants dive deeper in pursuit of their prey. The Greater Cormorant chases its prey under water, using its webbed feet for propulsion; when it catches a fish it surfaces and swallows it head first. Its slender, hooked-tip bill is well suited to holding on to captured fish.

Not surprisingly, cormorants are unpopular with fishermen, but a series of tests in Europe found that for every healthy fish the cormorant caught it took five suffering from parasites, so at least in one respect it actually helps fishermen by maintaining a healthy fish population and should therefore be regarded as a friend.

On Lake Naivasha the Greater Cormorant nests on dead trees standing in water, and very often the Speke's Weaver will build its nest hanging from the underside of the cormorant's.

43

Yellow-billed Stork

Mycteria ibis

This common and tame stork is found throughout East Africa, wherever there is water, and often congregates in pools which are drying out. It is often incorrectly called Wood Stork or even Wood Ibis: the Wood Stork is a bird of the Americas and although it is generally similar in appearance to the Yellow-billed, its bill is dark.

The Yellow-billed Stork usually feeds by walking slowly through shallow water with its bill submerged, relying on the bill's special tactile sensitivity to find prey. When the bill touches edible matter, it immediately snaps it up with what is believed to be the quickest muscular action in the animal world. Occasionally the bird can be seen stirring the mud with one foot while holding out one wing. Stirring the mud is obviously intended to disturb potential food items, but no one is sure why the wing is held out in this way, unless its purpose is purely to aid balance.

Little Egret

Egretta garzetta

At the start of the breeding season, the Little Egret grows splendid nuptial plumes called aigrettes, and during the early years of this century its worldwide population was depleted by hunters killing it for this plumage. The aigrette was very fashionable and widely used to decorate ladies' hats.

Since this practice has been discontinued the Little Egret's numbers have increased and it is once again common, usually found along the edges of swamps, lakes and seashores. It stalks its food in shallow water, occasionally dashing forwards or sideways with amazing agility as it sights its prey.

Although it is often confused with the Cattle Egret, its solitary feeding habits, black bill, and black legs with yellow feet should make it easy to distinguish.

45

Sacred Ibis
Threskiornis aethiopica

This striking black-and-white bird, widely depicted in Ancient Egypt in both carved and painted form, derives its name from the Egyptians' belief that their god Thoth sometimes came to earth in the form of a Sacred Ibis. Thoth, a scribe of the gods, was the inventor of writing and the measurer of time who symbolized wisdom and knowledge. He is often shown with a Sacred Ibis's head, an odd representation considering the naked head and neck are surely the least attractive part of the bird.

It seems likely that the Ancient Egyptians reared the Sacred Ibis in captivity, because of their reverence for the bird. In the temple complex of Saqqara, which dates from 2649–2575 BC, approximately one and a half million mummified remains have been found, many in enclosures and pens.

The religious significance of Thoth's incarnation as a Sacred Ibis was such that Herodotus, the Greek historian and traveller writing in the fifth century BC, noted that in Egypt the secular killing of this ibis, whether intentional or not, was punishable by death.

Interestingly, the Ancient Egyptians knew that the Sacred Ibis kept bilharzia (a debilitating disease) in check, but not how. We now know that a snail is the host of the bilharzia parasite, and snails, along with frogs and aquatic insects, form the major part of the Sacred Ibis's diet. Unfortunately, because of extensive swamp drainage and land reclamation over the years, the bird is now extinct in its ancient home and bilharzia is rampant.

The Sacred Ibis is also known to prey on the eggs and nestlings of other birds, and it is an opportunist scavenger, not even averse to cake, as anyone who has had tea on the lawns of the Lake Hotel, Naivasha, will know!

Masai Mara National Reserve

The Mara, Kenya's most spectacular game-viewing area, is world famous for its herds of plains game and its diversity and abundance of predators. It is also an exceptional place to see birds, the variety and profusion of its birds of prey being particularly alluring. Out on the open plains an eagle, vulture or Lilac-breasted Roller will be seen perched on almost any tree, while on the ground you are sure to see a variety of bustards, a stately, striding Secretary Bird or a large, turkey-like Ground Hornbill. Also to be observed in the grassland is the Yellow-throated Longclaw, which will remind American visitors of their own Meadowlark. Oxpeckers are a common sight, perched on rhino, buffalo and giraffe, and busily feeding.

In any of the numerous wet or marshy areas you might see a pair of Wattled Plovers or even majestic Saddle-billed Storks. In the woodland bordering the Mara River or one of its tributaries you may well catch a glimpse of a Ross's Turaco, one of the most beautiful of that striking-looking family.

There is nowhere better in East Africa to see vultures. They are a very common sight on the African plains and, although they are undoubtedly ugly and almost universally despised for their so-called repulsive habits, they do play a very necessary role, acting as a thorough waste disposal and sanitation system.

The main differences between vultures and eagles are the vulture's comparatively weak feet and predominantly scavenging habits; eagles need strong feet to enable them to kill their prey, although quite a number of them also scavenge.

Contrary to popular belief vultures are clean birds, bathing regularly and meticulously, particularly after eating. Most have bare heads, which are obviously easier to keep clean than feathered ones. After bathing they sit with their wings open and their backs to the sun to dry out.

Eight species of vulture occur in East Africa and, although there is a lot of competition between them, they all have slightly different habits. The first vultures to arrive at a carcass early in the morning are usually Hooded and/or White-headed. They may peck at the eyes and mouth of the dead animal, but are unable to open up the carcass. So too is the next to arrive, the Rüppell's, which will probably be closely followed by the White-backed; they will push the early arrivals out of the way and thrust their heads into the mouth and throat, and even the anus. Only when the large Lappet-faced Vulture arrives will the carcass be opened – the Lappet-faced can tear it easily with its powerful bill.

Because of their weight and size most vultures are unable to fly far without the help of warm air thermals, so it is very often not until after 8 a.m., when the air has started to heat up, that vultures are seen to soar in the air looking for food. (On one occasion when I was driving over the Serengeti plains at dawn, explaining this phenomenon to my clients, our vehicle was almost hit by two White-backed Vultures. They were struggling to fly from a nearby tree, in air still too cold to help them, to the remains of a wildebeest killed by lions during the night.)

When soaring vultures spot a carcass, they descend to it immediately, giving a signal to any other vultures in the vicinity. Films showing vultures circling over a dying man or animal are largely a Hollywood invention; when groups of vultures are seen circling it is usually because they are gaining height after feeding, or more often after they have bathed.

Of course, next time you are on safari you may well see a Lappet-faced Vulture flying at night, so that it can be the first at a carcass; and the last to arrive, on a thermal, will be a Hooded Vulture. On safari there is always something new just waiting to happen.

In the Mara you should also keep an eye open for Ostrich, Marabou, Egyptian Vulture, Bateleur, Tawny Eagle, Long-crested Eagle, Martial Eagle, Fish Eagle, Crowned Crane, Kori Bustard, Crowned Plover, Little Bee-eater and Black-headed Weaver.

Short-toed Snake Eagle (Black-chested Snake Eagle)

Circaetus gallicus

The large, yellow, owl-like eyes, the rounded head, bare legs and erect stance are typical features of this medium-sized eagle. It prefers lightly wooded country and open plains, and it is not uncommon in the Masai Mara National Reserve and adjoining Serengeti National Park in Tanzania. It is usually solitary, but sometimes a number will gather in an area where prey is plentiful; it will also occasionally roost in small groups.

As its name suggests, the Black-chested Snake Eagle (I prefer to use this name, which I think is much more descriptive, although it has officially been changed) feeds mainly on snakes, but it will also kill lizards, rats and mice. It has a very unusual hunting style for an eagle: it normally soars high in the sky when looking for prey – flying as high as 300 feet or more – but it will often hover like a giant kestrel. (Early one morning I was slowly stalking a snake which was lying on a rock in the sun, when a Black-chested Snake Eagle dropped on to it and flew away before I realized what had happened. My eye had been glued to the viewfinder of my camera, and yet I didn't manage to take a photo of either the eagle or the snake!)

If this eagle captures a small snake it will often carry its prey up into the air and pull it up between its claws with its beak before swallowing it. Large snakes are killed on the ground, torn up and eaten. When feeding young, the eagle may arrive at the nest with a half-ingested snake, which the chick pulls out of its throat, often with help from the parent.

The Snake Eagle is not immune to snake bites, but it is well protected by the thick down underneath its feathers, and by the heavy scales that cover its legs and feet.

Some African tribes believe that all eagles will attack their chickens, young goats or sheep, and the Black-chested Snake Eagle is sometimes killed as a consequence. In fact, because it feeds on snakes, it is very useful to man and should be protected everywhere, as indeed is the case with many other predators.

Lappet-faced Vulture
(Nubian Vulture)

Torgos tracheliotus

The largest vulture in East Africa, the Lappet-faced Vulture is the only one with a bill big enough and strong enough to tear open a carcass. It also has longer and stronger toes than other vultures and is capable of holding down large pieces of meat while it feeds. It is thought that the Lappet-faced Vulture can prey on small mammals, but there is little evidence of this, although it has been recorded killing flamingoes.

Its size, bill, completely naked head and the folds of bare skin on its head and face make it unmistakable. Because of its size it needs warm air thermals if it is to fly any distance, and is therefore usually the last of the vultures to reach a kill. When it does arrive it dives straight into the seething, squabbling group, breaking it up and driving off the other birds.

When threatening other vultures the Lappet-faced runs forwards, its head lowered and neck outstretched, with the feathers on its back erect, wings partly spread and tail cocked. It prefers to eat on its own, and will often remain on the outskirts of a group of feeding vultures, occasionally snatching food from them. This bullying behaviour has also earned it the name of King Vulture.

Hooded Vulture

Neophron monachus

The Hooded Vulture is a versatile scavenger, widespread and usually common, occurring in wooded country as well as open plains. It is also often found around traditional villages and, in West Africa, even in large towns and cities, where it has largely taken the place of the Black Kite as a general waste-disposal unit.

It is much smaller and lighter than most other vultures and, because it is not as dependent on air thermals for flight, it is often the first to arrive at a carcass. Later it will have to give way to other, larger birds. It is thought that other vultures may use the Hooded as an indicator: if it is not molested at a kill, it is safe for the rest to land.

The Hooded Vulture has a long, slender bill and usually feeds on scraps left by other vultures, though its bill enables it to pick flesh out of crevices inaccessible to the larger birds, and to extract larvae from the dung beetle's balls of dung. It can also hold meat in its feet and pull off pieces with its bill. Unlike many other vultures the Hooded is a clean feeder and does not emerge soiled from a kill.

The face of the Hooded Vulture can often be seen flushing red, apparently with excitement. This is thought to be a way of establishing dominance over others of its kind.

Saddle-billed Stork

Ephippiorhynchus senegalensis

This is the largest of the African storks, widespread but not common throughout East Africa. Either solitary or in pairs – it is thought to mate for life – it is usually found feeding in swamps, where its diet consists largely of fish and frogs. Occasionally when feeding it will throw its prey up into the air, catch and then swallow it.

The Saddle-billed Stork is spectacular in appearance, its name deriving from the bright yellow frontal shield on its huge bill. It also has a distinctive bright red naked spot on its breast.

Male and female are similar in appearance, but the female is about ten per cent smaller and has a bright yellow eye, while the male has a dark brown eye and two yellow wattles or lappets at the base of his bill.

Yellow-billed Oxpecker

Buphagus africanus

A familiar sight to any visitor to Africa, oxpeckers or tickbirds, as they are usually known, are unique to the African continent. Being highly specialized birds, dependent on wild game animals and domestic cattle, they are most frequently seen on rhino, buffalo and giraffe, though strangely never on elephant. Both Yellow- and Red-billed Oxpeckers eat mainly the parasites that live on these animals, but will also feed on dead skin and scar tissue. This keeps wounds open and vulnerable, which cannot be of benefit to the host animal, but in other respects the relationship between the animal and the oxpeckers is symbiotic. In addition to controlling parasites, the oxpeckers act as look-outs, warning their host of the approach of man (but not, apparently, of lion).

The oxpecker's bill is flat on either side and used in a scissoring action to pick ticks off the host animal. The birds have short legs, very sharp claws and a stiff tail, a combination which

enables them to climb all over the host's body rather like a woodpecker climbs a tree.

They nest in holes in trees, making their nests largely out of animal hair.

The two species occur throughout East Africa and are common in the national parks, but they have almost disappeared from cattle-ranching country since dipping became widespread and destroyed their food supply.

57

Denham's Bustard (Jackson's Bustard)

Neotis denhami

Wattled Plover

Vanellus senegallus

The most endangered bustard in East Africa, Denham's used to be common, especially in the Rift Valley, but it is now found only very locally and the population may still be decreasing. The reasons for the decline in numbers are not fully understood, but a combination of modern farming methods and the vast increase in the human population in areas where the Denham's used to be found has probably contributed to the problem.

It is a shy bird, but anyone driving into the Masai Mara Reserve by way of Aitong has a good chance of seeing it on the open plains where this photograph was taken.

The Denham's Bustard has an elaborate courtship display, in the course of which the male inflates his neck pouch and struts before the female – a most impressive sight.

This is a common bird in the Masai Mara Reserve, always found in pairs or small groups near the edge of swamps, in soggy grassland or by the side of temporary pools of water.

Surprisingly, it does not appear to breed in Kenya.

59

Ground Hornbill
Bucorvus cafer

This large, black, turkey-like bird is a frequent sight on the Masai Mara plains, and one of the delights of camping there is to wake up at dawn to its powerful, booming call. This call has given the bird a certain mystique among African tribes, and is interpreted by some as the female saying: 'I'm going, I'm going, I'm going home to my relations,' and the male replying: 'You can go home, you can go home, you can go home to your relations.'

A number of tribes either protect this hornbill or use its image as a tribal token.

The Ground Hornbill is the largest of its family, usually seen in pairs or small groups moving with its characteristic waddling gait over the grasslands, feeding on a variety of prey such as insects, lizards, frogs, mice and possibly snakes. Very often a female will have at least two males with her when feeding young. Although mainly terrestrial, the Ground Hornbill can fly with a very slow, heavy wing-beat, showing conspicuous white primary feathers. It also has the most beautiful long eyelashes.

African Marsh Owl

Asio capensis

You will often flush this owl when driving across country over the Mara/Serengeti grasslands. If you see it before it flies away, it will usually be crouching in a small hollow in the grass with its characteristic black eyes wide open and two small ear tufts raised in alarm.

The Marsh Owl lives in long grass and marshy areas and is often gregarious – the only owl that is. It is terrestrial, nesting and roosting on the ground, and is locally common, often seen flying around its territory or sitting on a convenient post several hours before sunset. If disturbed, it may well fly around in circles above the intruder's head.

The young leave the nest before they can fly and disperse to individual roosts, where they continue to be fed by the adults. Even so, there are records of young Marsh Owls being taken by Marsh Harriers and even by Verreaux's Eagle Owls.

Secretary Bird

Sagittarius serpentarius

'Why "Secretary Bird"?' is the first question anyone asks when we come across one of these striking-looking creatures on safari. Originally it was thought that the name came from the bird's resemblance to a Victorian secretary with a quill pen behind his ear: but a new theory is that it derives from the Arabic *saqr et-air*, which means 'hunter-bird' and which may have been corrupted into French as *secretaire*. You can take your pick as to which version you choose! As for the scientific name, *Sagittarius* is Latin for 'archer' (as in the sign of the zodiac) and *serpentarius* means 'interested in snakes'.

The Secretary Bird feeds mostly on grass-hoppers, beetles and other insects, but may also take small mammals such as mice and hares, which it kills with strong downward stamps of the feet before swallowing them whole. Sometimes it chases its prey with wings outstretched. If it discovers a snake, it spreads its wings and circles warily, striking carefully with its feet until it is sure the snake is dead.

Generally considered to be a terrestrial eagle, the Secretary Bird can soar to great heights, but is more usually seen walking over the grasslands, either alone or with a mate nearby. The strange, characteristic crest is normally flat, but at times appears to be blown upwards by the wind; it can also be raised when the bird is excited.

The Secretary Bird nests on top of quite low, flat-topped acacia trees, where it is very conspicuous.

Dark Chanting Goshawk

Melierax metabates

The Dark Chanting Goshawk is a common Mara resident, usually seen sitting on an exposed branch or termite mound, from which it makes short swoops on to its prey. Although lizards appear to be its favourite food, it will also take insects, mice and small birds. At times it will hunt on the ground, running after prey and looking like a miniature Secretary Bird.

The English name is translated from the French *faucon chanteur*, given to it by the explorer François Levaillant, who was struck by its melodious, chanting call. The call is made by both sexes, mostly in flight but also sometimes when perched, and is most frequently heard during the mating season.

Little Bee-eater

Merops pusillus

The Little Bee-eater is a widespread, common, tame and lively bird, generally found singly or in pairs not far from water. It usually perches low down on a bush or bare stick and will often have a favourite perch which it and its mate will use every day. It is always on the lookout for any flying insect. The moment it spots its prey the Little Bee-eater dashes off and there is an audible snap if the chase is successful. Then the bird returns to the same perch with a graceful glide. If the prey is a bee or wasp, the bee-eater will beat it and remove the venom by squeezing the prey's abdomen along the perch before eating it.

Sometimes the Little Bee-eater is found out on the open plains of the Masai Mara, and here it will use a rock or even tall grass for a perch.

African White-backed Vulture

Gyps africanus

This is the commonest vulture in East Africa and is found in most of the national parks and reserves. It roosts and nests in trees, often gregariously. Despite its name the white back can be difficult to see and is sometimes absent. The White-backed Vulture is very similar in appearance to the Rüppell's Vulture, but has a more uniform brown plumage, black bill and brown eye. Older birds sometimes have an almost white plumage.

The White-backed Vulture is usually unable to open up a carcass, despite the very sharp cutting edges of its bill. But once the carcass is open it thrusts its long, naked neck deep inside. It has a specially adapted tongue with backward-facing spines that are used to rasp off soft flesh.

This bird's soaring flight is wonderful to behold, but it cannot fly far without the aid of thermal air currents. Unless there is carrion nearby the White-backed Vulture may not leave its roost until early morning, when the air is warm enough to carry it. Then it sometimes eats so much that it is unable to take off again. Like most other vultures it likes to bathe after eating.

Lilac-breasted Roller
(Mosilikatze's Roller)
Coracias caudata

A common and conspicuous resident, occurring singly or in pairs and usually in open country, this is perhaps Africa's loveliest bird. Even someone who has never paid much notice to birds before cannot fail to appreciate its beauty, and I am sure it has converted more people to the joys of bird-watching than any other species.

During the last century Mosilikatze, king of the Ndebele tribe, in what is now Zimbabwe, declared that the feathers of the Lilac-breasted Roller were to be reserved for his exclusive use; some people call the bird Mosilikatze's Roller to this day. The 'roller' part of its name comes from the spectacular and noisy acrobatic display-flight the male performs during the breeding season.

The Lilac-breasted Roller is easy to see as it always perches very visibly on a dead tree, on top of a low bush or even on a roadside telegraph pole, whence it swoops down on to its prey, usually eating it there and then before returning, often to the same favourite perch. It is during this brief flight that it is seen at its most glorious as it reveals its incredibly beautiful and colourful wings.

It feeds on a variety of insects — locusts, grasshoppers, beetles — and also on scorpions and lizards. If it catches a large, hard beetle, it will often smash it against a convenient stone before eating it.

It nests in a hole in a dead tree and is very territorial during the breeding season, chasing away birds as large as the Martial Eagle.

Meru National Park

'Elsa country', Meru National Park was made famous by the book and film *Born Free*, the story of Elsa the lioness and the late Joy and George Adamson. Meru is still an area of largely unspoilt wilderness, so despite a network of generally well-maintained roads there is nevertheless a feeling of being in 'real' Africa. The park's attraction lies in the diversity of its scenery, with a variety of habitats ranging from forest, dry bush and grassland to swamps and numerous small rivers, lined with doum palms and other kinds of trees.

My favourite river in Meru is the Rojoweru. Here you have a very good chance of seeing the elusive African Finfoot and, if you are extremely lucky, the rare Pel's Fishing Owl. The Palm-nut Vulture is another uncommon bird found along the river; Meru is, I think, the only place in East Africa where it can be seen with any regularity.

During August and September the Madagascar Bee-eater breeds in colonies along the Tana River, probably the only known inland breeding site in Kenya of this beautiful bird. Colonies of Black-headed Weavers build their nests in the riverside trees, and along the river you are sure to hear the bubbling call of the White-browed Coucal.

Some of the birds commonly seen are the Somali race of Ostrich, White-backed Vulture, Pygmy Falcon, Martial Eagle, Fish Eagle, Pale Chanting Goshawk, Crowned Crane, Kori Bustard, Buff-crested Bustard, Namaqua Dove, White-bellied Go-away Bird, Lilac-breasted Roller, Rufous-crowned Roller, Giant Kingfisher, Little Bee-eater, Red-billed Hornbill, Blue-naped Mousebird, Paradise Flycatcher and Black-headed Weaver.

Variable Sunbird

Nectarinia venusta

This tiny, beautiful sunbird is a very common resident. It feeds on nectar from most flowering trees and plants, but seems especially fond of the flowering leonotis and salvia.

In north-eastern Kenya the male Variable Sunbird has a white belly, whereas in other parts of the country it is yellow-bellied. This difference probably explains its common name.

As with other species of sunbird the female is a dull, drab-coloured bird, in complete contrast to her mate.

When the main structure is complete, usually after two or three days, the male has to attract a female. He does this by hanging upside down beneath the nest, swaying vigorously from side to side with quivering wings and making excitable, swizzling sounds. If the male is unsuccessful in attracting a female, he will give up on that nest and start all over again. I have seen a male Black-headed Weaver knocking an abandoned nest to the ground, presumably so that he can use the same branch again for the next attempt.

If the male does succeed in attracting a female to his nest – and it appears that the female selects her mate purely on the quality of the nest he has built – she signals her acceptance by lining the nest with fine grasses.

Black-headed Weaver
Ploceus cucullatus

A common, gregarious bird, the Black-headed Weaver nests in colonies in bushes and palms along many of the rivers in Meru National Park, where the large number of their suspended nests is a feature of the landscape. In other areas of East Africa it nests in and near villages, and is often given the name Village Weaver.

The nest hangs from the end of a drooping branch denuded of foliage. The leaf-stripping is done by the male, as is the building of the nest itself: it is woven from blades of grass or palm fronds, which the male tears off by gripping them with his bill and then flying away with them.

Verreaux's Eagle Owl
Bubo lacteus

This huge owl occurs mainly in thick woodland or riverine forest and exhibits a liking for large trees. Verreaux's Eagle Owl can be confused with the Spotted Eagle Owl, but Verreaux's is much larger, has dark brown eyes (while the Spotted Eagle Owl has yellow eyes) and pink eyelids, and is generally paler in colour. In some parts of Africa it used to be called the Milky Eagle Owl, matching its scientific name.

Its characteristic deep 'hu-huhu-hu' call is a distinctive sound of the African bush, and it is probably because the cry sounds so mournful that the Verreaux's Eagle Owl is connected with so many legends and regarded with suspicion by a number of African tribes.

The Verreaux's Eagle Owl has a varied diet which may include hares, hedgehogs, hyraxes, bushbabies, frogs, snakes, guineafowl, francolins and even insects. It sometimes makes its nest inside a large hollow tree such as a baobab, but very often it will take over the stick nests of other birds and occasionally use the top of a huge Hamerkop's nest.

Chestnut-bellied Kingfisher

Halcyon leucocephala

Strangely, of the dozen species of kingfisher occurring in Kenya, only half are fish-eaters. The others belie their name and eat mostly insects. The Chestnut-bellied Kingfisher is one of these.

It is common in dry bush country and, although usually found near rivers and streams, it feeds mainly on large insects, beetles and even lizards, which are more numerous in the riverside bush. Like other kingfishers it also needs a bank such as a river bank into which to burrow to make its nest.

While on the look-out for prey the Chestnut-bellied Kingfisher sits very still in a bush or tree, usually in the shade. Often it is seen only when it flies away, displaying the brilliant blue of its wings.

Vulturine Guineafowl

Acryllium vulturinum

This handsome bird, with its cobalt blue chest and almost naked, vulture-like head, can be quite common in hot, dry bush country, where its shrill, cackling call is a familiar sound. It usually occurs in large flocks and can often be seen scratching the ground with its feet, searching for seeds.

Although it spends most of its time on the ground, it is a strong flier and roosts in trees at night.

If water is available it will drink daily, often from the same spot on a river bank or water-hole, but it can seemingly exist without water for a long time.

Guineafowl are often preyed on by Martial Eagles, and on one occasion I watched at close quarters a Vulturine Guineafowl being stalked and killed by a leopard.

Hamerkop
Scopus umbretta

The Hamerkop (or Hammerhead Stork) is one of nature's curiosities, taking its name from the characteristic silhouette made by its head and permanently erect crest. It is believed to be the king of all birds, and appears in more African legends than any other. The Hamerkop is sometimes called the Lightning Bird because it is supposed to be able to make rain; some witch-doctors suspend a Hamerkop above a dry river-bed during rain-making dances, to indicate the height to which they would like the river to rise. Certain tribes believe it is very bad luck to disturb this bird, while others have only to see a Hamerkop flying overhead for it to bring bad luck for the rest of the day, and still others believe the Hamerkop's appearance brings death.

The reason for all this is probably that the Hamerkop has a habit of decorating the top of its nest with bones, parts of animals, snakeskins, dead birds and pieces of cloth or plastic, giving the whole a rather macabre appearance.

The Hamerkop builds a huge nest, sometimes as much as six feet high and weighing 200 pounds. It will usually be in a tree near a water-course, but may also be sited on a cliff or kopje. The nest, which takes two to three months to complete, is made of sticks and lined with mud and is virtually impenetrable. The entrance, which for some reason very often faces east, is on the underside of the nest, making entry other than by flight particularly difficult.

While the nest is being built it is often visited by other species: legend has it that all the birds help the Hamerkop to build a vast nest fit for the king of birds, though it is more likely that the others are stealing nest material or trying to take over the nest. Another legend has it that there are three rooms inside a Hamerkop's nest – one for nesting, one for the nursery and one for dining – but in fact there is only one. However, one nest dismantled by researchers was found to be made up of over 8,000 items.

Despite all this effort the Hamerkop often loses its nest, sometimes before it has used it itself; a Verreaux's Eagle Owl or Egyptian Goose may make its nest on top, while a Barn Owl or Grey Kestrel may move inside.

The Hamerkop feeds on fish, tadpoles and frogs, which it always swallows head first. It will also take offal thrown away by fishermen. Its usual method of fishing is to walk slowly through shallow water, snapping up any creature it disturbs, but at times it will stand still, stirring the

mud with its feet until prey emerges. The Hamerkop will also fly low over water with its legs dangling, picking up any floating food and catching small fish.

Often when flying it makes a peculiar squeaky, whistling cry which doubtless also fuels the superstitions.

One final strange characteristic of the Hamerkop is its habit of standing on the back of another Hamerkop, usually during a dispute of some kind, uttering a peculiar, wavering, high-pitched cry.

Banded Snake Eagle

Circaetus cinerascens

The visitor to Kenya is most likely to see this uncommon eagle in Meru National Park, where it is usually to be found sitting alone in a tree near water; from this perch it can dive down on to its prey. Its diet consists of small snakes, mice, lizards, frogs and toads.

Like other members of its family it has large, yellow, owl-like eyes, a rounded head and bare legs.

There is no record of the Banded Snake Eagle breeding in East Africa, and it seems likely that it is a non-breeding visitor from other parts of the continent.

Palm-nut Vulture

Gypohierax angolensis

The rarest of the East African vultures, the Palm-nut Vulture is unique among birds of prey in that it is mainly a vegetarian. Because of this it is most often found along the coastal strip of East Africa, where it feeds on the husks of the raffia and oil palms.

Inland it is seen at Lake Jipe in Tsavo National Park and in Amboseli, but more commonly in Meru, where it breeds and where this picture was taken. Its diet appears to differ according to its habitat. At Lake Jipe it is known as a scavenger, feeding on dead fish, and in Amboseli I have

twice seen individual Palm-nut Vultures at a carcass. Perhaps because it is smaller than most other vultures the Palm-nut doesn't appear to contest a carcass with the larger and more aggressive birds, tending instead to pick up small pieces of meat dropped by them, as do the Hooded and Egyptian Vultures.

In Meru I have seen a Palm-nut Vulture eating crabs and on two occasions young terrapins, while elsewhere it has been recorded catching small fish by flying low over the surface of rivers and streams. Recently I saw one eating the meat put out to attract leopards at Samburu Lodge. After a bit of a struggle the bird managed to hold on to the suspended bait with its feet and hung upside down, flapping its wings for balance while it fed.

79

Black-headed Plover

Vanellus tectus

During the day, this distinctive crested plover is usually found, singly or in pairs, resting in the shade of an acacia tree or a bush. It feeds mainly at night, on insects.

In Kenya it occurs in the hot, arid thornbush country and, although it prefers to spend the day in the shade, strangely enough it frequently nests completely in the open under the hot sun. The

Black-headed Plover's nest, like the nests of other plovers, is on the ground and the eggs are laid in a scrape or hollow, often with just a few pieces of grass and small stones surrounding it.

As the temperature rises during the day the nesting bird crouches over the eggs to shade them from the hot sun – completely opposite behaviour to that of birds nesting in cooler climates. Very often the nesting bird looks distressed, with its bill open as it pants, its body feathers ruffled to circulate air and its wings held slightly away from its body to help dissipate the heat.

Madagascar Bee-eater

Merops superciliosus

This bird is usually present in East Africa between May and September, virtually replacing the Blue-cheeked Bee-eater in some areas. No one is certain where 'our' Madagascar Bee-eater spends the rest of its time. It used to be thought that it migrated from Madagascar, but there is no proof of this, and in fact the indigenous Madagascar Bee-eater is present throughout the year in Madagascar.

It has recently been discovered breeding in the banks of the Tana River in Meru National Park during August and September, and indeed Peter Jenkins, who was warden there for many years, believes that this is an annual event. There are thought to be several distinct populations of Madagascar Bee-eaters living in various parts of Africa, and it even seems likely that the population breeding along the banks of the Tana River is independent of the one at Baringo: the Baringo birds don't leave there until September, by which time the Tana birds are already breeding.

Although the Madagascar Bee-eater is often found near swamps and rivers, and among the mangroves on the coast, it can also live far from water and may be seen feeding in small flocks in dry bush country.

Bateleur

Terathopius ecaudatus

The majestic Bateleur in flight, with its long wings and stumpy tail, is yet another of the unforgettable sights of the African skies. It seldom flaps its wings, but rocks them from side to side (*bateleur* is French for tightrope walker or acrobat). With a speed of 30 to 50 miles an hour it can cover 150 miles a day over the open savannahs. It is easy to distinguish the sexes in flight – the male has a broad black band along the trailing edge of his wing, and the female a much narrower one.

The tail of the mature Bateleur is so short and stumpy that its feet extend beyond it in flight, but the all-brown juvenile has a long tail. It takes seven or eight years for a Bateleur to attain its adult plumage, and its tail shortens with each moult.

Although usually solitary, the Bateleur can be very sociable, gathering together in large numbers: I once counted a group of twenty-six on the Serengeti plains, near Lake Ndutu. It bathes regularly and afterwards sunbathes with its wings held in a heraldic position.

The Bateleur is primarily a scavenger, but it has been recorded killing dik-dik, mongooses, and game birds: swooping down steeply on its prey and killing it on the ground. This switch to hunting small game often occurs when the bird is feeding young in the nest, and ensures that the chicks have sufficient calcium. The Bateleur will also eat fish, locusts and termites when available. Its feet have roughened soles which also enable it to grasp snakes and lizards.

Nairobi National Park

Nairobi National Park is unique: the main entrance is only fifteen minutes' drive from the city centre and, although the park is not much more than forty-four square miles in area, it contains a large variety of animals and has a wide diversity of habitats – highland forest, open plains, rocky gorges, riverine acacia forest and a number of dams. With this range of terrain it is not difficult to understand why more species of birds have been recorded in this tiny area than in the whole of Great Britain.

The Crowned Eagle nests in the forest, and along the forest tracks you should see the White-eyed Slaty Flycatcher and the occasional Northern Olive Thrush and Baglafecht Weaver. On the open plains you will see the Ostrich, Secretary Bird and a hovering Black-shouldered Kite.

For me the highlight of a visit to Nairobi National Park is a visit to the Hippo Pools. Here you are allowed to walk along a track on the banks of the Mbagathi River. If you are quiet and careful you may see a pair of the rare African Finfoot. The vegetation – especially the yellow-barked acacia – is usually alive with birds and you are almost certain to see the shy Green-backed Heron, the Malachite Kingfisher and Grosbeak Weaver.

Other birds frequently observed include the Great White Egret, Cattle Egret, Egyptian Goose, Secretary Bird, White-backed Vulture, Tawny Eagle, Martial Eagle, Crowned Eagle, Long-crested Eagle, Bateleur, Augur Buzzard, Lilac-breasted Roller, Malachite Kingfisher, Cinnamon-chested Bee-eater, Paradise Flycatcher, Blue-eared Glossy Starling, Superb Starling and Variable Sunbird.

Holub's Golden Weaver

Ploceus xanthops

This large weaver does not nest colonially like most others of its family, but is usually found in pairs or small groups. The male is particularly elegant with his upper chest and throat washed with orange and his distinctive pale eye. The female is similar in appearance but does not have the orange wash.

The Holub's Golden Weaver prefers damp areas and occurs in tangled bush and reeds bordering rivers, swamps and marshes. The male builds a nest overhanging the water.

Speckled Mousebird
Colius striatus

Mousebirds are endemic to Africa; they are fruit-eaters and considered a pest by farmers as they do serious damage to their crops. They get their name from their soft hair-like plumage and their habit, when feeding, of creeping and running about in bushes and trees, more like mice than birds. Instead of perching like other birds, they hang from a branch with their feet level with their heads. They even sleep in this position, often in a small group with their heads together.

All mousebirds have short legs and long, curved claws. It is characteristic of the family that the outer toe on either side of the foot is reversible, able to move backwards and forwards, which enables the bird to run rather than hop along branches.

Mousebirds may be co-operative breeders, with non-breeding adults helping to feed the young of other birds in the same small group; certainly on a number of occasions I have watched several adult mousebirds all feeding one or two young at the same time. Some birds even help others build nests and incubate eggs, but this has not been proved to be the case with mousebirds.

When disturbed, mousebirds take flight one after the other. After a few short, fast wing flaps they glide to the next bush, into which they crash, hanging on for a few moments before disappearing inside.

The Speckled Mousebird is the most common of the family, found almost everywhere in East Africa where the habitat is suitable, but particularly in the Highlands and wetter areas. It can frequently be seen sunbathing on an exposed branch at the top of a bush, especially in the early mornings.

Helmeted Guineafowl
Numida meleagris

A familiar and common bird of East Africa's national parks and reserves, the Helmeted Guineafowl usually occurs in large, noisy flocks, busily scratching the ground searching for seeds and insects. It spends most of its time on the ground, but roosts in trees at night and will also fly up into trees if chased by a predator. When alarmed it can be extremely vociferous, a warning which may be useful when travelling or camping in the African bush.

Although the Helmeted Guineafowl is highly gregarious, its flocks sometimes several hundred strong, pairs go off on their own at breeding time and do not rejoin the group until their young are independent.

Male Helmeted Guineafowl are extremely aggressive and chase one another with their wings held at a characteristic angle, higher than normal and tight against the body: this makes them look larger from the side but much slimmer from the front. In his book *The Leopard's Tale*, Jonathan Scott likened guineafowl to motorized tea-cosies – an apt description!

Its speckled body, bright blue head and striking helmet make the Helmeted Guineafowl conspicuous when feeding out in the open, but when it stands still in the shadow of a bush it is very effectively camouflaged and can be almost impossible to spot.

Black-headed Heron

Ardea melanocephala

Confined to Africa south of the Sahara, the Black-headed Heron is a common bird, usually solitary except when roosting or breeding, and generally found far from water, hunting in open country or grasslands. It is quite at home on dry land and feeds on a variety of prey, including mole rats, rats, mice, grasshoppers, lizards and frogs; its control of pests is much appreciated by farmers.

When feeding it walks slowly through the grasslands, head held well forward. If it spots prey it often moves its head slowly from side to side, possibly to help it judge distance; then it suddenly thrusts its head forward and captures its prey.

The Black-headed Heron often breeds in towns and villages and there are nest colonies near Kisumu, in Njoro High Street, in Malindi and Entebbe – and in the railway yards of Nairobi! Interestingly, if this heron breeds away from towns and villages, it will do so in a mixed colony with other herons.

Bronze Sunbird
Nectarinia kilimensis

This large sunbird – the male is eight inches long, including his tail – is a common sight in Nairobi gardens. It occurs in highland forest edges and clearings and, like other sunbirds, feeds mainly on the nectar of flowering plants and trees, but will on occasion hawk for insects. Unlike most others of its family the Bronze Sunbird will often spend considerable time hovering, mainly because it is too heavy for its weight to be supported by the plants it likes to feed on.

Here, a Bronze Sunbird is seen feeding on a *Cuphea eximia* – a plant with no common name – in my garden. If you look carefully you will see that as it hovers it turns its head upside down, making it much easier for its long bill to penetrate into the base of the flower.

Crowned Crane
Balearica pavonina

One of East Africa's most beautiful birds, the Crowned Crane is usually found in open country or on the edges of swamps and marshes, where it feeds on a wide variety of items, including insects, frogs, vegetation and seeds. It is thought to mate for life and is usually found in pairs or small groups, though occasionally it gathers in large flocks.

Its familiar loud, melodious and evocative cry, normally given in flight, is unforgettable and may explain why some African tribes hold this crane in superstitious regard. Some believe that the Crowned Crane brings rain, while others, including the Masai, incorporate its nuptial ritual into their own dances. This mating 'dance' is a wonderful sight: a pair of cranes, sometimes a group, will suddenly start to hop and jump gracefully about each other with their wings partly spread. Then they open their wings fully, bow to each other and jump several feet in the air. On landing they run round each other and start all over again.

At breeding time a pair of cranes will move into a swamp or marsh, where they build a nest mound on the ground. These days, many swamps and marshes are being drained and the land is being reclaimed for agricultural purposes. This, added to the fact that the Crowned Crane is a popular attraction in zoos and parks throughout the world and is therefore often the victim of an illegal trade, means that its future is far from certain. It would be a very sad day for Africa if the sight and sound of the Crowned Crane were to disappear for ever.

Pin-tailed Whydah

Vidua macroura

The Pin-tailed Whydah is a common and well-known little bird, at least in the breeding season, when the male with his distinctive black-and-white plumage and long tail can be seen with groups of dark brown females and immature males.

Out of the breeding season the male Pin-tailed Whydah is a drab brown bird, just like the female, except that he usually retains his red bill. But in his breeding plumage he is a pugnacious creature and seems to spend most of his day chasing away other birds, even kinds as large as a dove. For the rest of the time he performs his characteristic display, 'dancing' jerkily in the air over the perched female. With all this activity he hardly seems to have time to feed and rest, and must burn up a tremendous amount of energy during the breeding season.

The female builds no nest but lays her eggs, sometimes several, in the nests of other birds such as waxbills. I also strongly suspect that the Singing Cisticola is an important host, at least in the Nairobi area. The adult whydah takes no part in the rearing of its young. The whydah chicks hatch and, in marked contrast to the young of the notorious cuckoo, grow up with the young waxbills and seem to share both nest and food supply amicably. The young of the two species closely resemble each other – even the patterns inside their gape (beak) are similar – so it is possible that the adult waxbills are unaware of the intrusion.

Eurasian Bee-eater

Merops apiaster

It is often said that European birds are rather dull compared with African birds. The Eurasian Bee-eater is surely an exception, with its rich chestnut-brown head and shoulders, its pale golden back and rump, bright yellow throat and green-blue belly and chest.

Because the Eurasian Bee-eater spends most of its time flying high in the air or sitting in tall trees, it is easy to overlook its true attractiveness. Only on the rare occasions that it is seen at close quarters can its beauty really be appreciated.

A common migrant, it passes through East Africa in large flocks from September to November, on its way to southern Africa. Your attention is drawn to it by a far-carrying, pleasant, liquid call, usually a chorus from many birds as they hawk insects. This is one of the calls that the Rüppell's Robin Chat most likes to mimic, and it does it so well that I have often been fooled into thinking a flock of these bee-eaters was close by.

During March and April it stops off again on the journey north. At this time it is very common in the Nairobi area, where flocks roost in the tops of very tall trees, and in the early morning can often be seen sunbathing on bare branches.

The Eurasian Bee-eater feeds on bees, butterflies, moths and locusts, but it is not a popular bird in some parts of Europe. Whatever its faults – bee-keepers hate it – it seems a crime that so-called 'hunters' in southern Europe kill up to 5,000 of these birds every year in the name of sport. Unfortunately it is also the victim of bird-limers, who spread a sticky lime on branches to enable them to catch the birds for food.

There is a small breeding population of Eurasian Bee-eaters in South Africa which breeds during October and November, just as the Eurasian migrants are arriving. After breeding these African birds migrate northwards at the same time as the Eurasian ones. This has led to speculation that they could, in fact, be Eurasian birds breeding in both northern and southern hemispheres. As all these birds are identical in appearance it is very difficult to prove or disprove what would be a unique event, but most experts maintain that there are two quite distinct populations.

Ostrich

Struthio camelus

The Ostrich is the world's largest living bird. The male is a little bigger than the female and can often be as much as eight feet tall, weighing about 300 pounds. It is usually found in small groups feeding among the plains game, and is sometimes preyed upon by lions, hyenas and wild dogs. Although it is flightless it manages to survive because of its acute alertness, a running speed of up to forty miles an hour, and a deadly powerful kick. It has been known to attack man if provoked. I once approached, in my Land Cruiser, a pair of Ostriches which had a group of almost fully grown immatures with them. The female suddenly dashed aggressively towards us but turned away just short of the vehicle. I edged a little closer, but was still at least fifty yards from the group when the female again ran towards us, hissing fiercely, and stopped only when she reached the vehicle, her head almost inside the window.

At other times when a potential predator approaches, the Ostrich lies low with its neck extended along the ground. It is probably this behaviour which gave rise to the myth that the Ostrich buries its head in the sand, and led to the idiomatic phrase referring to someone who refuses to admit to reality.

The Ostrich feeds mainly on vegetation, seeds, flowers and succulent plants, but will also eat insects such as beetles – and I once saw a male Ostrich swallow something that appeared to be a small rodent. It also swallows stones, which probably help it to digest seeds. These stones are highly prized by the Masai who find them, usually highly polished, in the stomachs of dead birds.

The Ostrich is unusual among birds in that its feathers, having no barbules, are loose and fluffy. It also has no preen gland (oil from the preen gland is essential for flighting birds to keep their feathers in good condition). Although it is flightless it does have small wings which are used for balance when running, and for shading its eggs; and of course their most dramatic use is during the Ostrich's display, which must rival anything seen at the Folies Bergères.

A unique feature of the Ostrich is that it has

only two toes on each foot – no other bird has fewer than three.

The male is normally monogamous but will be polygamous if the opportunity arises. He defends a large territory in which his mate will lay a clutch of four to eight eggs in a scrape in the ground. Other females – and apparently not necessarily ones which have mated with the territorial male – will also lay their eggs in the same place, so there may eventually be as many as thirty or forty eggs, each equal in size to twenty-four domestic hens' eggs, in the one nest.

As with most ground-nesting birds the Ostrich does not begin to incubate eggs until the clutch is complete: this ensures that all the young hatch at the same time.

During the incubation period the mainly black male incubates at night, while the brown and less conspicuous female incubates during the day. The Ostrich normally feeds only in the daytime, so the female doesn't actually start her incubation stint till a few hours after dawn, and in the evening the male will usually relieve her before dark, thus allowing her to feed quickly at either end of the day.

The young Ostriches are nidifugous – able to leave the nest soon after hatching, like a domestic hen's chick – and can run and feed almost immediately.

The reasons for many females laying their eggs in the same nest are not clear. But among many theories, one is that the number one female keeps her eggs in the centre of the nest while incubating, leaving those laid by other females on the outer edges and therefore more vulnerable to predators.

Grosbeak Weaver
Ambylospiza albifrons

This is a big weaver with the large, thick bill characteristic of the family. The predominantly black male has distinctive white patches on its forehead and its wings; the female is dull brown and streaky.

The Grosbeak Weaver lives in small colonies in swamps or in dense vegetation near water, and is locally common. Most species of weaver build hanging nests; the Grosbeak is distinguished by its practice of slinging the nest between usually two, sometimes three, vertical reed stems. The nest, built by the male, is finely woven from thin grass strips and is oval in shape with an entrance near the top. The male is also thought to build extra nests with larger entrances, apparently to be used for roosting. I suspect, however, that these additional nests are merely ones that the female has rejected.

Among other weaver species, if a female accepts a nest, she lines it and shapes the entrance to her own satisfaction. This may well be true of the Grosbeak Weaver too.

Long-crested Eagle

Lophaetus occipitalis

The Long-crested Eagle is a small eagle that no-one should have any problems identifying. With its long, floppy, almost comic-looking crest, it is unmistakable. Even in flight its black-and-white barred tail and white 'window' patches on the wings are distinctive.

The Long-crested Eagle is found in most of Kenya except the very dry areas. It prefers to hunt in light woodland, forest edges or from trees along watercourses. It is usually quite tame and can be observed sitting patiently on an open branch or even a fence or telephone post, from where it can drop onto its prey. The Long-crested Eagle should be protected if only because it preys mainly on rodents, making it a friend to man.

Lake Nakuru National Park

Lake Nakuru is world-famous for its spectacular flamingo population; at times well over a million are resident. Africa's best-known ornithologist, the late Leslie Brown, described Nakuru as 'the ornithologist's Serengeti', and Roger Tory Peterson considered it 'the world's most fabulous bird spectacle'. It is a sight that I never tire of.

Lake Nakuru was made a national park in 1961, the first place in Africa to be so designated primarily for the benefit of birds. The lake is surrounded by large areas of open grassland, beautiful acacia woodland and rocky outcrops. With such a varied habitat it is not surprising that over 400 bird species should have been recorded there.

Although in some years, due to varying climatic conditions, the flamingo population drops quite dramatically, there are other attractions for the bird-watcher. There might be thousands of White Pelicans and Greater Cormorants feeding on tilapia – the *Tilapia grahami*, a small fish introduced as an anti-mosquito measure – while along the edge of the lake thousands of wading birds, many of them migrants from Russia and Eastern Europe, feed busily.

Whenever I visit Nakuru I go to the Baboon Cliffs. From the cliff top there are marvellous views over the lake and surrounding country, and, if you take your lunch there, you are sure to see various chats and the Blue-eared Glossy Starling competing with the rock hyrax for scraps of food. You may also have wonderful views of the Augur Buzzard and Verreaux's Eagle as they soar alongside the cliffs.

Among the other birds more commonly seen are the Little Egret, Marabou, Yellow-billed Stork, Sacred Ibis, African Spoonbill, Crowned Eagle, Long-crested Eagle, Kittlitz's Sandplover, Black-winged Stilt, Speckled Mousebird, White-eyed Slaty Flycatcher, Blue-eared Glossy Starling and Superb Starling.

White-fronted Bee-eater
Merops bullokoides

Usually found in small groups along dry ravines or river banks, this beautiful bee-eater often gives away its presence with its harsh, noisy call. It feeds on butterflies, bees and other flying insects. It nests colonially, sometimes in flocks several hundred strong, digging its nest burrow near the top of a steep river bank or cliff.

The White-fronted Bee-eater enjoys one of the most complex societies recorded among birds. At least two-thirds of the nesting pairs in a breeding colony will have non-breeding birds helping them; one or two helpers is the norm, but some nests have been observed with as many as five. These helpers may be previous offspring not yet ready to breed themselves, or other adults which have failed to breed for some reason. A group consisting of a nesting pair and its helpers forms a clan within the colony. Members of each clan will feed in the same area, help dig the nest burrow, feed the young and defend the nest from other bee-eaters and any predators. Nests attended by helpers have, of course, a much higher breeding success rate.

Birds love to sunbathe and the White-fronted Bee-eater is no exception. It can often be seen, usually by the entrance to its nesting hole, with its wings and tail outspread, feathers raised, head held to one side and eyes closed, apparently oblivious to the world.

Fish Eagle

Haliaeetus vocifer

The best known of all the African eagles, the strikingly conspicuous Fish Eagle is common on most lakes and rivers and in coastal areas. Its familiar ringing call evokes nostalgia in all Africa-lovers: I cannot think of a better way to be woken in the morning than by a pair of Fish Eagles in duet nearby. Although most frequent in the early morning, the call may be heard at any time of day, often with neighbouring pairs joining in, each proclaiming its own territory. The Fish Eagle calls with its head thrown back, both when perched and in flight.

Usually seen in pairs, perched on a vantage point at the edge of a lake or river, the Fish Eagle watches out for prey swimming just below the surface of the water. When it sights a suitable fish it makes a shallow dive and, at the last moment, throws its feet and talons forward to grasp the prey; it then continues its flight carrying its catch, to be eaten at a favourite perch. Occasionally the bird will flop into the water after grabbing a large fish, then use its wings to paddle back to the shore. The Fish Eagle has roughened soles to its feet, which help it hold on to its slippery prey.

On the East African soda lakes, where there are only the tiny *Tilapia grahami*, the Fish Eagle preys on both Greater and Lesser Flamingoes. It used to be thought that it took only young or sick birds, but it has now been recorded killing many healthy ones too.

It is also a pirate, chasing other birds, including other Fish Eagles, herons, storks and even Pied Kingfishers, until they either drop or disgorge their prey.

107

White Pelican

Pelecanus onocrotalus

The highly gregarious White Pelican is common throughout East Africa in the shallower lakes which contain fish. It even occurs at Lake Nakuru, which, being a soda lake, does not support a native fish population; the pelican feeds on the tiny but numerous tilapia.

It is one of the world's largest flying birds and much more numerous than the similar Pink-backed Pelican, though they are often found together. Although in adult plumage the White Pelican is white and the Pink-backed Pelican grey, the immature birds are confusingly alike. I find the easiest way to tell them apart is to study the pattern formed by the feathers above the bill.

In the case of the White Pelican the pattern comes to a point above the bill, while the Pink-backed's form a broad arc.

They also differ in their roosting and nesting habits: the White Pelican roosts on the ground, on the banks of lakes, and its nesting colonies are usually on sandy or rocky islands; the Pink-backed both roosts and nests in tall trees.

It is rare to find the White Pelican nesting in either Kenya or Tanzania, though nesting colonies have been found on rocky islands in Lake Elmenteita in Kenya and it is known to breed occasionally at Lake Rukwa in southern Tanzania. Some years ago I discovered a huge colony at Bahi Swamp in central Tanzania too. But for the most part they appear to nest further north, in the lakes of the Rift Valley of Ethiopia.

It is a remarkable experience to watch a colony of White Pelicans catching fish. While swimming, usually in shallow water, they form a horseshoe shape with the open end to the front. Then, rhythmically and in unison, they dip their heads into the water, while at the same time slowly tightening the semi-circle until a group of fish is trapped. Here the pelican's most remarkable feature, its large pouched bill, comes into play, acting like a huge net scooping up the fish.

The rhyme 'A wonderful bird is the pelican/Its beak can hold more than its belly can' has given rise to a widely-held belief that the pelican carries food in its bill. Unfortunately, this just isn't true. When it is feeding young the parent pelican will regurgitate food for its chicks; and the chicks in their impatience often push their heads right down inside the parent's throat to seize the food.

The White Pelican is a powerful flier, and a group soaring effortlessly in formation high in the sky, when moving from lake to lake, is a wonderful sight. This was particularly well illustrated when they bred at Lake Elmenteita, which contains no fish: the sky between Lakes Elmenteita and Nakuru was always full of pelicans.

The White Pelican, like many other birds, takes great care of its feathers and seems to spend hours preening. It has a special preen-gland at the base of its tail and it is oil from this gland, smeared over the feathers with the pelican's awkward-looking bill, that helps keep it in top condition.

Greater Flamingo

Phoenicopterus ruber

The Greater and Lesser Flamingo both occur on the East African soda lakes, and manage to co-exist because of their differing food requirements. The Greater Flamingo is mainly a lake-bottom feeder, tending to walk slowly through shallow water with its head submerged and bill filtering the mud, though sometimes it will stand in one spot and stir the mud with its feet. Occasionally it will swim out into deeper water, and to reach the mud at the bottom has to upend itself like some ducks. Its bill – with fewer and coarser laminae than that of its smaller relative – allows it to consume quite large food items; it usually preys on small snails, crustacea and aquatic invertebrates, but will also eat the blue-green algae favoured by the Lesser Flamingo when they are abundant.

The Greater Flamingo is much larger than the Lesser, some males growing to a height of six feet or more, and can also be distinguished by its paler plumage, bright scarlet wing coverts and black-tipped pink bill. It is by far the rarer of the two species and, to my mind, much the more beautiful.

It is not confined to the Rift Valley soda lakes, but occurs regularly for short periods and in smaller numbers at Lakes Baringo and Naivasha, and also along the coast, particularly at Mida Creek, south of Malindi. It is possible that these coastal birds are migrants from Europe or Asia, where the Greater Flamingo also breeds, but this has yet to be proven.

The nuptial display involves a loosely-knit group of Greater Flamingoes suddenly stretching their necks upwards, pointing their bills skywards while at the same time flicking their heads from side to side; then suddenly snapping their wings in and out in a salute.

The Greater Flamingo's main breeding area appears to be Lake Natron in Tanzania, where it and the Lesser Flamingo build similar mud nests next to one another. Occasionally it breeds on rocky islands in Lake Elmenteita, where the nest consists of a few sticks, grass and feathers laid on the bare rock.

Unfortunately, the nesting Flamingoes at Elmenteita have frequently been badly disturbed. Once a colony of White Pelicans – much larger, heavier birds – moved on to the islands to breed themselves, and on other occasions the mere presence of Marabous has been enough to unsettle the flamingoes.

In some years they have also tried to breed at Lake Nakuru, but, because there is as yet no policy of protecting breeding areas from disturbance, tourist vehicles driving up to within a few yards of the birds have forced them away from their nests.

Lesser Flamingo

Phoeniconaias minor

The gathering of thousands, sometimes hundreds of thousands, of flamingoes on Lake Nakuru is a magnificent sight. It is common to see the lake completely surrounded by a pink band of feeding flamingoes, and very often there are thousands more swimming on the lake itself.

The Lesser Flamingo is a surface feeder, eating mainly microscopic cells of the blue-green alga called Spirulina. Its bill is a specially adapted filtering structure. The lower mandible (which becomes the upper when the head is bent over during feeding) is light and acts like a float, keeping the bill at a certain depth. Both mandibles are lined with bristly lamellae which act as filters, and the tongue works as a pump. As water is drawn into the bill the lamellae lie flat, but as the water is pumped out they become erect, retaining the Spirulina. When feeding, whether standing or swimming, the Lesser Flamingo swings its head from side to side, drawing food from the top layer of water only. It has been estimated that flamingoes extract as much as sixty tons of algae a day from Lake Nakuru.

I went into a health food shop in a Nairobi suburb recently and saw bottles of Spirulina for sale as a tonic – imported all the way from Mexico!

The late Leslie Brown aptly described the Lesser Flamingo's pre-breeding display as a 'communal stomp'. Groups of flamingoes among the feeding flocks look much darker red than usual and appear to be crushed very close together, walking with their heads held high. The neck feathers are erect, the necks 'blushing brightly'. Occasionally they will snap out a wing in a sort of salute, or lower their heads on to their breasts as if their necks were broken, while all the time their legs are taking rapid short steps, giving the impression of a forest of red, twinkling legs.

Breathtaking though this sight is, the Lesser Flamingo is perhaps even more beautiful in flight. It tends to fly from lake to lake at night, possibly to avoid predators such as eagles; and to

hear a flock overhead is yet another of the unforgettable experiences of camping in Africa. During the day it flies mainly to different feeding areas, but also searches for fresh water which it needs both for drinking and for bathing, an activity it seems to enjoy immensely. At Lake Bogoria the only fresh water regularly available is from hot springs, but this doesn't seem to bother the flamingoes, despite the fact that the temperature is as high as 65 to 70°C (150 to 160°F).

The Lesser Flamingo's main breeding site is the almost inaccessible and inhospitable Lake Natron in Tanzania, but occasionally it also tries to breed at Lakes Bogoria and Nakuru. At Lake Natron it builds nests of mud and soda eight to sixteen inches high, and although the temperature of the surrounding mud may be as high as 55°C (about 130°F), the temperature in the nest cup is much lower at around 30 to 35°C (85 to 95°F). This temperature drop is thought to be caused by capillary action through the nest mounds: water soaks up through the porous nesting material and cooling occurs when the water evaporates.

The Lesser Flamingo's main predators are Tawny, Steppe and Fish Eagles and Marabous, but it can also be threatened by jackals and hyenas.

Samburu and Buffalo Springs National Reserves

This is harsh, arid bush country, bisected by the wide, shallow and muddy Ewaso Nyiro River. The scenery is dramatic, with a hazy backdrop of mountains and hills, including the impressive, sheer-sided Lolokwe. Along the river there are large stands of beautiful riverine forest which, unfortunately, are slowly being destroyed by elephants. Also along the river, and along many of the dry water-courses, is the characteristic tree of these north-eastern areas, the doum palm, the only palm in the world with a divided trunk.

Even though the environment is harsh, birdlife is prolific, with birds of prey being particularly abundant. Here the tiny Pygmy Falcon, possibly the world's smallest bird of prey, and the 'uncommon' Somali Bee-eater are often seen. Another feature of the area is the nest of the White-browed Sparrow Weaver; there can be few trees in either reserve that don't have nesting colonies of this bird. If you happen to be in the vicinity of Buffalo Springs look carefully at the sparrow weavers, as it is here that the very scarce Donaldson-Smith's Sparrow Weaver occurs. It has a very limited range, almost entirely restricted to this one area south of the Ewase Nyiro River.

The Lilac-breasted Roller is quite common here, as is its duller-looking cousin, the Rufous-crowned Roller. But the birds that are perhaps most representative of Samburu are the hornbills. There never seems to be a moment during the day when you cannot hear or see a Red-billed Hornbill, or the larger and much less common Yellow-billed Hornbill.

Other birds you are likely to note include the Somali race of Ostrich, Cattle Egret, Egyptian Goose, Rüppell's Vulture, White-backed Vulture, Lappet-faced Vulture, Martial Eagle, Bateleur, Spur-winged Plover, Mourning Dove, Emerald-spotted Wood Dove, Chestnut-bellied Kingfisher, White-throated Bee-eater, Little Bee-eater, Red-billed Hornbill, Red and Yellow Barbet, Superb Starling and Hunter's Sunbird.

Kori Bustard
Otis kori

The Kori Bustard is Africa's heaviest flying bird; the male is thought to be close to the theoretical maximum weight for a flying bird. It usually flies only when pressed, but when it does so it is an awesome sight.

It is usually found singly, walking across open grasslands, but tends to seek shade at midday and will often be seen standing under a bush or small tree. It also occasionally occurs in very loose groups. Like other bustards it is omnivorous, feeding on a wide variety of insects, seeds, fruit and even flowers.

The male's display is remarkably stately, whether he is standing still or walking along slowly. His neck inflates, exposing white under-feathers. His chest is thrust forward, head held high, tail cocked upright touching his head, and wings drooped. From a distance it is hard to believe that this is a bird. Sometimes he adds to the effect by uttering a strange, booming call.

The Kori Bustard is still quite common in East Africa, although the demands of farming and the expanding human population threaten part of its range. However, it is perhaps most at risk from those who export it illegally to the Middle East for sporting purposes.

Yellow-billed Hornbill
Tockus flavirostris

This is another bird that lives in the dry bush country of East Africa, and although not common it can often be seen in the Samburu and Buffalo Springs National Reserves. The Yellow-billed Hornbill seems to eat just about anything – fruit, insects, mice, lizards and even the occasional small bird. It has been observed following foraging bands of mongooses, ready to snap up insects or small mammals escaping from them. In fact the mongooses derive some protection from the hornbill, as it will give warning of any approaching predator such as the Pale Chanting Goshawk.

It is easy to recognize the Yellow-billed Hornbill in the air by its characteristic undulating flight with periods of gliding between wing flaps.

It also has the strange nesting habit unique to hornbills: a suitable hole in a tree is selected and the female is walled up inside by means of mud and droppings, leaving only a small slit through which the male feeds her. During incubation, the female goes through a complete moult, so if anything untoward happens to the male she is doomed. As the young grow bigger she breaks out of the nest so that she can help the male with feeding the chicks. After the female has left, the young instinctively repair the hole so that once again only a small slit is left.

Because the female starts incubating immediately the first egg is laid, and there may be several days between the first and last egg, the chicks hatch at different times and are different sizes. Shortly after the female leaves the nest, the oldest and largest chick is ready to do the same and starts to chisel its way out, using its strong bill. At the same time, the smaller chicks will be trying to repair the damage. Eventually the largest chick manages to break out and almost immediately has to make its first flight. Meanwhile, the remaining chicks are busy repairing the hole again, with no help from the parents. Each of the young hornbills leaves the nest, one at a time, in this labour-intensive way.

White-headed Vulture

Trigonoceps occipitalis

The White-headed Vulture is an uncommon but distinctive bird and, for a vulture, rather a beautiful one. It usually occurs singly, but an adult may sometimes be seen with a juvenile. Because its wings are a little shorter and broader than those of most large vultures, it is able to fly much more easily without the aid of thermals and is often one of the first to arrive at a carcass, along with the smaller Hooded Vulture. It is a clean, 'outside' eater, never seen besmirched by blood or entrails like most other vultures. In fact it tends to feed on leftover scraps, behaving rather like a much larger version of the Hooded Vulture.

In addition to the normal carrion, the White-headed Vulture is known to feed on termites. The pastoral Somali people of northern Kenya say it will kill dik-diks, hares and guineafowl, but this has never been confirmed by an ornithologist.

It is a comparatively timid bird and, despite its size, is frequently chased away by other vultures; it is also very easily disturbed by tourist vehicles.

Gabar Goshawk

Melierax gabar

This small goshawk looks like a miniature version of the Pale Chanting Goshawk, but their habits are very different. The name Gabar is thought to be a Hottentot word bestowed upon it by François Levaillant.

The Gabar Goshawk is common in acacia woodland and dry thornbush country. Its nest in a bush or small tree is very often covered with spiders' webs, and it is likely that the goshawk puts the spiders in the nest while it is building it. Some nests become completely covered, which makes for superb camouflage.

This goshawk is a bird killer, its usual habit being to sit in a tree by a water hole waiting for suitable prey, which may be a bird as big as itself. It catches its prey in its talons after a swift pursuit through the air. It will rob the nests of weaver birds and Quelea, hanging upside down and flapping its wings as it pulls the nestlings out with its beak. Insects, lizards and small snakes also form part of its varied diet.

In its normal colouring, the Gabar Goshawk has a very distinctive white rump, most clearly visible in flight and a useful aid to identification. Melanistic (black) colouring is not uncommon and makes for a very smart-looking bird.

Blue-naped Mousebird

Urocolius macrourus

Like its more common relative the Speckled Mousebird, the Blue-naped occurs in flocks and family groups, but it prefers the drier areas of East Africa. It is a much slimmer and smarter bird than the Speckled, and normally draws attention to its presence with a strange 'pee-e-e' call as it bursts out of a bush.

White-browed Sparrow Weaver

Plocepasser mahali

Although this is a plain-looking bird, it is one of my favourites. It is noisy, conspicuous and gregarious, and its pale yellow, untidy nest and constant calling will always remind me of safaris in Africa. A pair builds several nests – from dry grass – at the end of branches, often on the west side of a bush or tree. Most of the nests are used for roosting and have two entrances, facing downwards. When breeding, the female will seal off one entrance and line the chamber.

Pearl-spotted Owlet
Glaucidium perlatum

One of East Africa's smallest owls, this is a locally common bird occurring in dry bush country, and because it is diurnal it is more often seen in the national parks than any other. Typically, it will be found sitting quietly in an acacia tree or being mobbed by other birds.

The Pearl-spotted Owlet often occurs in the same areas as the Pygmy Falcon, which is similar in size, and the two species have a number of behavioural features in common. Their flight is almost identical, and when perched they both periodically bob their heads and wag their tails up and down or from side to side. The surest way of identifying the owlet is by its cry – a series of rising notes, followed by a descending one – often heard during the daytime.

It feeds mainly on beetles, grasshoppers and termites, but will also hunt and eat rats and mice. There are even records of this tiny owl catching doves and other birds as large as itself. It nests in abandoned woodpecker and barbet holes.

Owls are famous for their ability to turn their heads almost completely round, and the Pearl-spotted Owlet is no exception. When its head gets three-quarters of the way round – 270 degrees from the front – it will rapidly swivel it in the opposite direction and continue to scan its surroundings. On the back of its head are two marks which look very like eyes, the purpose of which is obscure.

Namaqua Dove
Oena capensis

This delightful, tiny dove is at times very common, usually seen in pairs or small groups searching for food on the ground. It seems to prefer dry, sandy areas, but occurs almost everywhere in Kenya apart from the cooler Highlands.

The Namaqua Dove perches low in bushes, and may build its nest almost at ground level. Its flight is low and fast, displaying cinnamon-coloured wings. After landing it will often raise its tail and slowly lower it again.

The male differs from the female in having a black face, throat and chest.

125

White-bellied Go-away Bird

Corythaixoides leucogaster

A dull-looking member of the turaco family, the White-bellied Go-away Bird is common in dry bush country (unlike its brighter-coloured relatives, which all live in forests). It gets its name from the all-grey Go-away Bird of southern Africa, whose loud call could be interpreted as 'Go away'. Both species call when disturbed, and, of course, often gave the call when a hunter – native or modern – was approaching an animal, which was thus alerted to danger and could run away. When calling, they also raise and lower their crests.

The White-bellied Go-away Bird is usually seen in small groups, flying from bush to bush. Often when landing it raises its tail up over its back, almost as if it were having balance problems.

It is a fruit-eater and can often be seen in the gardens of various lodges in the national parks, feeding on fruiting trees and shrubs.

Pale Chanting Goshawk

Melierax poliopterus

This common resident of Samburu is very similar to the Dark Chanting Goshawk, but as it occurs only in dry bush habitat east of the Rift Valley there should be no confusion. As its name suggests, it is paler than its relative, but a more reliable distinction is the colour of the cere and legs: in the Dark Chanting Goshawk they are both red, while in the Pale they are yellow.

Like the Dark, the Pale Chanting Goshawk is usually seen perched on a prominent tree or termite mound from which it swoops down to catch its prey. Its diet is again very similar to that of the Dark Chanting Goshawk, but it has been observed catching birds in flight and is also capable of catching young African hares.

Pygmy Falcon

Polihierax semitorquatus

Another resident of dry bush country is Africa's smallest bird of prey, which measures a mere seven or eight inches from the tip of its bill to the tip of its tail. It is usually seen sitting on the tops of small trees or on open branches of large trees from which it can scan the ground for prey, often bobbing its head up and down as it does so. Insects make up the major part of its diet, but it will also prey on lizards and small snakes. From a distance the Pygmy Falcon looks just like a shrike, and is easy to miss.

It is usually found in pairs; the sexes are very similar in appearance, but the female can be distinguished by her rich brown back.

The Pygmy Falcon has the extraordinary habit of roosting and nesting inside the nest of a White-headed Buffalo Weaver, and is very rarely found anywhere that the weaver does not occur. Despite the fact that the falcon sometimes catches and eats birds as large as itself, it is thought that the weaver tolerates the usurper because it is a deterrent to snakes, which often raid weaver nests.

Somali Bee-eater

Merops revoilii

A common resident of the dry bush country in eastern Kenya, this small bee-eater has a large, stout bill and dull plumage, and somehow never looks neat and tidy like other members of its family. Solitary pairs are usually seen perched in low bushes or trees, waiting for passing insects.

The Somali Bee-eater normally fills the same niche in the hotter, drier parts of Kenya as the Little Bee-eater does in other areas of the country, but both can often be seen in close proximity in the Samburu and Buffalo Springs National Reserves.

Although there are only two records of this bird breeding in Kenya, I have seen a pair excavating a hole in the ground in Buffalo Springs, and on another occasion I found a pair feeding young in Samburu.

Tsavo East and West National Parks

These two areas, divided by the main Nairobi–Mombasa road, make up one of the largest national parks in the world. Together they cover nearly 8,000 square miles – an area larger than Wales. Although both parks consist mainly of arid bush country, there is still a great diversity of habitat. In the Kilaguni Lodge area there are large lava flows, some many miles long and probably less than two hundred years old; by contrast, among these flows stand the strange-looking and mysterious baobab trees, many of which are thought to have been there at the time of Christ. The famous Mzima Springs issue from one of these lava flows; the spring water, crystal clear, eventually supplies the town of Mombasa, some 150 miles away. Around the springs the dense vegetation and palm thickets are a haven for birds, and you can expect to see the Long-tailed Cormorant, Darter, Black Crake, White-browed Coucal, Pied Kingfisher, Malachite King-fisher and Little Bee-eater.

Not far from Mzima Springs is Ngulia Lodge, where every year, particularly in November and when the clouds are low at night, thousands of migrant birds from Europe and Asia are attracted to the lodge's bright lights, which shine over a water-hole. Here, after all the tourists have gone to bed, and with the permission of the lodge's owners, teams of enthusiasts, mainly from the Ornithological Sub-committee of the East Africa Natural History Society but occasionally with helpers from all over the world, set up fine mist-nets to catch the migrant birds so that they can ring them. Birds ringed here have been discovered as far afield as Leningrad to the north and Malawi to the south.

During the spring migration (in March and April) the whole of Tsavo teems with Eurasian Rollers.

In the south-west corner of Tsavo is Lake Jipe, a beautiful, slightly alkaline, freshwater lake, with the impressive backdrop of Kilimanjaro to the north-west and, across the lake in northern Tanzania, the North Pare Mountains. Dense floating vegetation around the shore line creates small, waterlily-covered lagoons, where the Pygmy Goose, Jacana and even the Lesser Jacana, rarely recorded in Kenya, can be observed. This is also a wonderful place to see a variety of ducks, geese, kingfishers and herons, particularly the Black Heron. Recently a new lodge has been opened on the shores of Lake Jipe, which will be much appreciated by anyone wishing to make the most of this area.

Other birds commonly seen include the Ostrich, Grey Heron, Goliath Heron, Great White Egret, Cattle Egret, Squacco Heron, Yellow-billed Stork, Rüppell's Vulture, White-backed Vulture, Lappet-faced Vulture, Tawny Eagle, Black-chested Snake Eagle, Grasshopper Buzzard, Bateleur, Fish Eagle, Pale Chanting Goshawk, Helmeted Guineafowl, Black Crake, Crowned Crane, Lilac-breasted Roller, Pied Kingfisher, Malachite Kingfisher, Blue-cheeked Bee-eater, Little Bee-eater, Yellow-billed Hornbill and Buffalo and Golden Weavers.

Two-banded Courser

Rhinoptilus africanus

This is an uncommon bird, usually occurring in pairs or family groups in hot open country and arid, sandy, bush areas, where it can apparently survive without drinking water. It is mainly nocturnal and crepuscular, feeding at night and at dawn and dusk on insects and termites; its drab, mottled plumage is wonderful camouflage and the bird is often noticed only when it is running away. It relies so heavily on its camouflage that, if it rains, it moves out of the area before the grass grows too tall and green.

It has a weak, piping call, particularly when disturbed; you can often hear this cry as the bird flies overhead on moonlit nights.

The Two-banded Courser seems very reluctant to fly. It is often found along vehicle tracks but, instead of flying away when a vehicle approaches, it runs, flying only at the very last moment and then landing in front of the vehicle. It will do this time and time again, especially if the grass is long on either side of the track. Eventually it will fly to one side or behind the vehicle.

It makes no nest but lays a single egg among stones or animal droppings. Because it lives in hot, dry areas, the adult shades the egg rather than incubating it, and the pair frequently has to take it in turns to stand over the egg while the other adult cools off in the shade of a bush. Although the Two-banded Courser lays only a single egg, it compensates by breeding more than once a year.

Martial Eagle
Polemaetus bellicosus

This distinctive, magnificent, powerful but shy eagle is found in open woodland and forest strips adjacent to open country, although it is not very common anywhere. It is Africa's largest eagle.

It spends most of its day soaring high in the sky or sitting in the very tops of tall acacia trees. It has long toes and sharp talons especially adapted for catching fast-moving prey in open country, and although it feeds mainly on gamebirds such as guineafowl and francolin it will also take monitor lizards, hyraxes, ground squirrels, mongooses, dik-dik and the young of larger antelope. I once found a Martial Eagle mantling over a Kori Bustard, a bird considerably larger than itself, which it had almost certainly killed. Although it often kills large prey, the Martial Eagle, unlike the Crowned Eagle, is unable to dismember and cache it away from other predators.

The Martial Eagle builds a large nest high in a tree, and the female lays a single egg. The same nest may be used over and over again for a number of years.

Eurasian Roller

Coracias garrulus

A common and beautiful migrant from Europe and Asia, passing through on its way to and from southern Africa, the Eurasian Roller can usually be seen singly or in small loose groups; occasionally in April it appears in its thousands and there seems to be a roller sitting on the top of every bush and tree.

Its migration is a long one, taking eight or nine months. It leaves its breeding grounds in late summer, passing through East Africa in October and November, and eventually arriving in southern Africa in late December. In due course it turns round and heads north again, stopping off in East Africa in the spring. By April many of the birds have attained their brilliant breeding plumage and are quite a sight to see.

The arrival of the Eurasian Roller tends to coincide with the rains, when there are more insects available, and consequently there is less of a conflict than there might otherwise be between it and the resident African rollers.

The Eurasian Roller has typical roller habits and is usually seen perched conspicuously on exposed branches or posts, or on top of small bushes. From any of these perches it will dive down on to grasshoppers, termites and occasionally small rodents. It also has the harsh cry that is characteristic of the rollers, and a strong hooked bill.

African Pygmy Goose

Nettapus auritus

The world's smallest duck, the Pygmy Goose weighs just ten ounces. It is an uncommon, shy bird, preferring secluded pools covered with water-lilies, where it is found in pairs or small groups. Its most attractive plumage is a perfect camouflage, making it very difficult to spot as it remains motionless among the water-lilies.

Its name must be attributed to its goose-like bill, adapted to deal with the ripe seeds of water-lilies, which are its main food, although it also eats other aquatic vegetation, insects and probably small fish.

True geese mate for life, are ground nesters and never perch in trees, but the Pygmy Goose, by contrast, finds a new mate every year, roosts in trees, and nests in holes in trees or in the abandoned nests of Hamerkops.

African Spoonbill
Platalea alba

A common bird of the Rift Valley lakes, where it occurs in small groups, the African Spoonbill is also found at most lakes and swamps, coastal estuaries and lagoons. A group of birds can often be seen resting on the shore, all standing on one leg with their heads and bills tucked back under their wings. Once airborne, the African Spoonbill is a graceful flier and a group will often fly in V-formation.

The African Spoonbill is classed with ibises and they usually nest in colonies together. When the baby spoonbill hatches, its bill is the same shape as any other bird's, but as the chick grows, its bill gradually lengthens, and by the time the bird is fledged, the bill has developed the characteristic bulbous tip and spoon-like shape.

This clumsy-looking bill has an extremely sensitive inner surface. When searching for food, the spoonbill walks through shallow water, sweeping its bill from side to side in a scything motion, with its lower mandible raking through the bottom mud. It senses fish and other aquatic creatures instantly and traps them between its broad mandibles; it then lifts its head and tosses its trapped prey into the back of its throat.

Great White Egret
Egretta alba

The largest of the white egrets, this is a shy and usually solitary species. It occurs almost all over the world, and in the United States is called simply the Great Egret.

In the breeding season it grows long, nuptial plumes which were much prized by the plume trade in the early years of this century; indeed, in many parts of the world its population was wiped out. It was in an attempt to discourage the use of feathers for purely decorative purposes that a group of women met in Manchester, England, in 1889 – a meeting which led to the foundation of the Royal Society for the Protection of Birds. A few years earlier the Audubon

Society had been founded in the USA for similar reasons, and it chose the Great Egret as its emblem.

The Great White Egret occurs in swamps, lakes, marshes and also along the coast. It can usually be seen wading slowly, often up to its belly, leaning forward with its neck outstretched. If it sights prey, it will draw its head and neck back into a distinctive S-shape, before quickly striking down at its victim. It feeds on fish, aquatic animals and insects.

The Great White is often confused with the Yellow-billed Egret because the Great White also has a yellow bill in the non-breeding season, which is most of the year. In the breeding season the bill turns black. The Great White Egret is a much larger and longer-necked bird than the Yellow-billed, but perhaps the best way of telling the two species apart is by the long black gape line which extends well behind the eye in the Great White but stops just short of the eye in the Yellow-billed.

Because of their very long legs, herons and storks – the order to which egrets belong – need to be able to fly very slowly, particularly when coming in to land at their nest or in a tree for roosting: they experience the same problem as modern jet aircraft. The aeroplane solves it by extending the leading edge slats on its wings and extending flaps downwards from the trailing edge of the wing, giving it more lift and so delaying the stall. Herons and storks do something very similar. The alula or 'bastard wing', a group of feathers on the 'thumb' of the wing, is particularly large in these birds. If it is in danger of stalling, the heron or stork raises the alula so that it can almost hover as it lands. It is estimated that the alula can increase lift by as much as twenty per cent, and tests have shown that some birds are unable to take off if the alula feathers are cut.

Black Heron
Egretta ardesiaca

The Black Heron occurs only in Africa and is a local and uncommon bird. It prefers shallow water on the edges of lakes, swamps and mangroves and can usually be seen at Lake Jipe and at Mida Creek south of Malindi, where it is mostly found in small groups. Single birds do occur more or less throughout its range, but particularly at Lakes Nakuru and Naivasha.

With its striking blue-black plumage and bright orange-yellow toes, the Black Heron is unmistakable, especially if you observe it fishing, when it adopts its characteristic umbrella stance. Its fishing methods are unique, and, particularly if more than one bird is fishing at the same time, an unforgettable sight. The bird walks forward a few steps, lowers its head, then rapidly stretches its wings forwards and down until the tips of the feathers are almost touching the water. It holds this position for a few seconds while it snatches up its prey – small fish, aquatic insects and crustacea – then snaps its wings back, takes a few more steps forward and repeats the whole procedure.

The Black Heron's flight feathers are broader than normal, helping to form a better canopy. This shading must help the heron see more clearly into the water, but it is possible that it also attracts small fish into the shade. Strangely, the Black Heron has been observed 'canopying' on dull days and even at night, and one captive bird was seen to canopy over a plate of food, so it would appear that this behaviour is instinctive.

Jacana (Lily Trotter)

Actophilornis africanus

The Jacana, or Lily Trotter as it is also known, is usually found in pairs or small groups on lakes, swamps or ponds covered in water-lilies or other floating vegetation. There can be few more delightful sights in Africa than that of a Jacana gracefully and delicately stepping over the lily-pads, stopping occasionally to feed. Its extra-long toes help to distribute its weight over a large area, so that it appears almost weightless as it walks over the floating leaves. It usually finds food by pulling the lily-pads or vegetation over with its beak, then holding it down with a foot as it searches for aquatic insects and larvae.

The Jacana can fly quite strongly but, with its long legs and toes trailing behind, it looks ungainly and completely out of its element.

The breeding behaviour of the Jacana is very interesting, the females being polyandrous, mating with several males and leaving each male to

incubate the eggs and even rear the young on his own. The beautifully coloured but well camouflaged, pyriformed eggs are laid on a patch of floating vegetation. The eggs are almost certainly waterproof and have a high gloss finish, as if they had been varnished.

The Pheasant-tailed Jacana of Sri Lanka is known to move its eggs through open water, sometimes several yards, to a new nest site if the existing site is threatened, and it is likely that the African Jacana does so too. Certainly, while the male is incubating he will often lift the eggs clear of the damp nest by pushing his wings under them.

The insides of the Jacana's eggshell are white and very conspicuous to a potential predator, so when a chick hatches the male immediately flies off with the shell, dumping it some distance from the nest site. Within a few minutes of hatching the chicks are able to run around and feed for themselves, although they are very vulnerable to predatory birds and even some fish.

If the male Jacana wants to move from the nest for any reason – in search of food or to avoid a predator, perhaps – he calls all the chicks to him; they climb up and hide under his wings. The male then quickly walks away, as if alone, with only the dangling legs and toes giving a clue to the chicks' presence. This protective behaviour is thought to be unique to the Jacana.

The reasons for polyandry are not completely clear but, as Jacana chicks are very vulnerable and their survival rate is low, this probably ensures that enough chicks survive to become adults and reproduce in their turn.

Superb Starling

Spreo superbus

This is East Africa's most common starling, occurring in most areas of Kenya in a variety of habitats, and is very aptly named. It is brilliantly coloured, bold and gregarious, usually feeding on the ground on insects and berries.

Around game lodges it has become extremely tame – perky, cheeky and apparently quite fearless, often feeding out of people's hands.

Marabou
Leptoptilos crumeniferus

The Marabou, with its bare head and neck and its hunched appearance when standing, must take the prize for East Africa's ugliest bird; but even so it is majestic in flight, soaring easily on its eleven-foot-span wings. At times it has a long naked pink pouch hanging from its throat, apparently connected to its left nostril; the purpose of this is unclear. It also has on its upper back a bare skin sac which is normally hidden under its ruff but which inflates at times and becomes a bright orange-red colour, possibly when the bird is excited or in breeding condition.

The Marabou is omnivorous, its diet ranging from termites, frogs, fish and small mammals to animal carcasses and even flamingoes. It can be seen around game-viewing lodges in the national parks, waiting for food scraps, and is also a regular visitor to rubbish dumps near towns and large villages. It will accompany vultures at a carcass and, although it is much larger than most vultures, it will usually stand apart, only dashing in occasionally to grab small pieces of meat that the other birds have dropped. Long after – often days after – the vultures have finished with a carcass, the Marabou can still be found picking away at the bones.

Both the Greater and the Lesser Flamingo are regularly killed by the Marabou. Its strategy seems to involve herding flocks of flamingoes into deeper water, where they have difficulty taking off, and then flying at them. In the ensuing panic it is easy for the Marabou to stab a victim.

Strangely, considering the prevalence of the Marabou, there are very few known nesting sites. It nests colonially in tall trees or on cliffs, and when breeding it seems to be more particular about its eating habits, restricting itself to fish, frogs, insects and small mammals, possibly to ensure that the young eat an adequate and balanced diet with lots of calcium to aid growth.

The Marabou is normally silent, although the sound of it clattering its bill may be heard around its nesting colonies.

The Coast

The village of Watamu, north of Mombasa, is an ideal centre for anyone wishing to combine an oceanside holiday with a little birding. Down the road at Gedi are the ruins of a fifteenth-century Islamic town. The excavated ruins are set among lowland forest, which is a wonderful place to watch birds. Over a hundred species have been recorded here, including the shy and elusive African Pitta and Spotted Ground Thrush. Fifteen miles north of Watamu is the resort of Malindi, whose beach is good for terns, gulls and migratory waders; just north of Malindi the mouth of the Sabaki River also supports an abundance of waders, as well as less common birds such as the Malindi Pipit and Madagascar Pratincole. Back towards Watamu is the Sokoke Forest Reserve, covering an area of about 150 square miles, where you might see more rare birds such as the Amani Sunbird, Clarke's Weaver and, most uncommon of all, the Sokoke Scops Owl, which occurs in this forest and nowhere else.

On the eastern side of the Sokoke Forest is one of my favourite birding areas, Mida Creek. This is an expanse of tidal mud flats fringed with mangrove. Although it is rewarding at almost any time of the year, Mida is at its best during March and April when thousands of migrant Eurasian waders, many in their breeding plumage, gather in this rich feeding area. Among these waders you might see the Crab Plover, a migrant from its breeding grounds just north of the Kenya border in Somalia. In the creek itself there is often a small flock of Greater Flamingo, while among the many egrets and herons you are sure to see the distinctive Black Heron.

The area around the creek is a good place to look for the Senegal Plover, Broad-billed Roller, White-throated Bee-eater and an occasional Grasshopper Buzzard. Other birds commonly seen include the Great White Egret, Little Egret, Fish Eagle, Pied Kingfisher and a variety of plovers and sandpipers.

Little Stint

Calidris minuta

This is a small, common migrant, a highly gregarious wading bird. It occurs in small groups or flocks and can usually be seen busily feeding in shallow water. It walks quickly with its head down, probing rapidly with its bill, and hardly ever looking up. At times, particularly in April when the male must feel the breeding season and the need to establish a territory approaching, he can be very pugnacious, but doesn't usually fight for long before he resumes feeding.

The Little Stint breeds in the high Arctic tundra and birds ringed in Kenya have been recorded as far away as Khazakstan in the USSR.

Carmine Bee-eater

Merops nubicus

There can be few more instantly recognizable birds than this brilliantly-coloured bee-eater. It is a highly gregarious bird, and the sight of a gathering at its nest colonies or roosts – sometimes numbering thousands of individuals – is unforgettably spectacular.

In East Africa it excavates its nest burrow on flat ground in the Lake Turkana region during April and May. After breeding, the colony disperses, but by November flocks have gathered along the coast north of Mombasa. They stay there till March, usually roosting in their thousands in Kilifi and Mida Creeks, where they create quite a tourist attraction.

The Carmine Bee-eater feeds mainly on flying insects, locusts and bees. It has also been recorded diving into rivers for small fish, and is thought to be able to remove the venom from a bee in flight, although this has not been proven. It is well known for its appearance at bush fires, feeding on insects fleeing from the flames. In the Gambia the Carmine Bee-eater has been given a name that means 'cousin of the fires'.

Another familiar feature of the Carmine Bee-eater is its habit of perching on the backs of animals such as goats and sheep; it has even been seen perching on a Kori Bustard. The bee-eater is undoubtedly using the animal as a beater, catching any insect it disturbs. It is more usual for it to forage from a high perch – the top of a tree or even a telephone wire.

There is an unproven theory that, while the Carmine Bee-eater's plumage is brilliant to the human eye, it may be less visible to the insects on which it preys.

Grasshopper Buzzard

Butaster rufipennis

A visitor to eastern parts of Kenya from November to February, the Grasshopper Buzzard breeds from Senegal in West Africa across to Somalia in the east. In Kenya it occurs singly or in small groups, usually in open country, where its most distinctive features are the reddish flight feathers very noticeable when the bird is on the wing. It frequents bush fires and recently burnt ground, where it feeds on insects escaping from or caught by the fire.

Its numbers seem to have declined in recent years, which could be the effect of large-scale aerial spraying of pesticides, intended to control locusts but also fatal to other insects in the immediate area. As the Grasshopper Buzzard feeds mainly on grasshoppers and mantids, this spraying may be damaging to its food supply.

Usually a tame and approachable bird, the Grasshopper Buzzard is most often seen perching on low branches from which it can drop down on to its prey.

Crab Plover

Dromas ardeola

The pied plumage and large, powerful bill make the Crab Plover unmistakable. It is not a true plover, but belongs to a family all of its own.

A visitor to the Kenyan coast from August to April, it usually occurs in small groups, preferring open sand and mud-flats, and is most frequently seen at Mida Creek. Its diet consists largely of crabs and its long, strong bill is specially adapted for crushing them.

The Crab Plover breeds along the Somali coast and, very unusually for a wading bird, digs a nest burrow which may be as long as five feet. It lays a single, very large, white egg. The chick, very unlike a plover in its habits, is highly dependent on its parents for food.

Sokoke Scops Owl

Otus ireneae

Africa's smallest owl, a beautiful bird only six inches in length, is found exclusively in the Sokoke Forest near Malindi and must count as one of the world's rarest owls. It was not discovered until 1965, and tragically its survival is threatened because of forest clearance in its restricted habitat.

It can be identified quite easily at night by its distinctive call, very like that of a tinkerbird.

12 *Lake Magadi*

At last we come to Lake Magadi, my favourite of the Rift Valley alkaline lakes and a most fascinating place. Although it is not a national park, a visit here is essential for any keen birder. From Nairobi the journey south, only seventy miles along good tarmac roads, is interesting both scenically and ornithologically – so much so that it often takes much longer than you might expect to reach Magadi itself!

Soon after leaving Nairobi the road climbs to approximately 7,000 feet up the southern shoulder of the Ngong Hills (of *Out of Africa* fame). There are splendid views into the Rift Valley and, on a clear day, you can see both Kilimanjaro and Shomboli, a mountain on the southern shore of Lake Magadi.

From the Ngong Hills the road descends in a series of steps towards Magadi through interesting dry bush country and past dry river-beds. Forty miles from Nairobi lies Olorgesaille National Park, a prehistoric archaeological site developed by Dr Louis Leakey and his wife Mary. This site is a wonderful area for observing birds, particularly the Red and Yellow Barbet, Blue-naped Mousebird and Beautiful Sunbird. There is simple, thatched accommodation for anyone wishing to stay at Olorgesaille (book at the National Museum in Nairobi).

Finally, at the end of the road, at an altitude of 2,000 feet, lies Lake Magadi, the most alkaline of the Rift Valley lakes. Here the soda is mined and is an important export for Kenya, earning valuable foreign exchange.

The tarmac road ends and a sometimes rough track follows the western shore of the lake to Bird Rock and beyond. Bird Rock usually has a few Yellow-billed Storks sitting on it and is a good place to stop and look for a Chestnut-banded Sandplover – or Magadi Plover, as it is known locally – usually seen dashing about at the water's edge, snapping up insects and their larvae. Lake Magadi is the only place in Kenya where this bird is regularly found. Out on the lake you are sure to see flamingoes and Little Egrets feeding in the rich water.

Just beyond Bird Rock the track veers off to the right and carries on to the southern end of the lake. This part of the lake is fed by hot springs and is usually the richest area for birds. The Common Pratincole and Kittlitz's Sandplover regularly breed here, and so occasionally does the graceful Avocet. During the European winter this area teems with visiting Eurasian wading birds, the Little Stint most prevalent among them.

The arid bush surrounding Lake Magadi is good bird country – the attractive White-throated Bee-eater being just one bird that lives here.

A word of warning to anyone intending to visit Magadi: take plenty of drinking water and spare fuel, and be especially careful when driving over the soda flats as they are often deceptively soft and can be treacherous.

White-throated Bee-eater

Merops albicollis

The White-throated Bee-eater prefers dry, semi-desert country and although it is mainly a visitor to East Africa, appearing in September and October, there is a small, apparently isolated population which occurs in the Lake Magadi–Olorgesaille area all year round, breeding from April to June.

Its spectacular courtship flight, known as a "butterfly" display, is performed by several birds flying close together, alternating short, shallow wing beats and glides with wings held high. The display is accompanied by clamorous calling. The bird can also be seen perched with its wings held high, again calling vociferously.

Although it is a very gregarious bird, particularly when migrating, the White-throated Bee-eater's nesting colonies are very loose and spread out. The nest burrow is excavated on flat ground, usually in the lee of a grass tussock or even a small dead branch. The White-throated Bee-eater has a highly developed system of co-operative breeding, with up to ninety per cent of nests recorded as having from one to five helpers, almost all of them male.

154

Kittlitz's Sandplover

Charadrius pecuarius

The Kittlitz's Sandplover is a tame species common on inland lakes, sometimes occurring at the coast and even on airstrips. It seems to prefer alkaline lakes with large expanses of open land nearby and is usually found in loose groups, busily feeding on the ground on small insects and larvae.

It usually makes its nest scrape in soft sand or earth, not very far from water, and lays two eggs. If a human approaches a Kittlitz's Sandplover on its nest, the sitting bird immediately starts kicking sand and earth over the eggs to cover them, before running quickly away. When the danger has passed it returns to the nest and partly uncovers the eggs again. The reason for this behaviour is not completely clear, but as the Kittlitz's Sandplover nests in open spaces under the hot sun the action does, at the least, serve to provide some shade for the eggs. What remains obscure is why the bird does not react in the same way when an animal approaches: it is apparently only a human intruder that provokes this behaviour.

Avocet
Recurvirostra avosetta

This graceful wading bird is the emblem of the Royal Society for the Protection of Birds: the creation of suitable conditions for the Avocet to breed in Britain after an absence of more than thirty years was one of the Society's early success stories.

In Kenya the Avocet occurs on most of the soda lakes, and is thought to be resident, as there is no evidence of Palaearctic birds coming so far south. In some years, a small population of Avocets breeds on the soda-flats on Lake Magadi.

Common Pratincole
Glareola pratincola

A gregarious, tame and at times very common bird, the Common Pratincole prefers open ground near lakes, rivers and coastal estuaries, where it often occurs in large flocks. It has a noisy but graceful, fast, swallow-like flight and could be taken for a giant swallow.

Although it feeds mainly in the air on termites and other insects, it also spends a lot of time feeding on the ground, where it looks very tern-like. Sometimes it stands still, only its head moving as it snaps up small passing lake flies, but at other times it runs along the ground pecking at insects and beetles.

It nests in large colonies on open, flat ground, laying two or three eggs in a scrape, often among animal dung or rocks for camouflage.

Chestnut-banded Sandplover (Magadi Plover)

Charadrius pallidus

The tame, tiny, neatly marked Chestnut-banded Sandplover is confined to the lower altitude lakes in East Africa, and Lake Magadi is the only place where it is found in Kenya. Here it is a common resident and can usually be seen feeding on small lake flies and their larvae, along the water's edge.

It breeds in the cooler months of July and August, and its nest, if you can call it that, is just a slight scrape in the soft soda. It lays two eggs, which strike me as being very large in proportion to the size of the bird; these are often laid among stones or pieces of soda, which appear to form a sort of decoration.

Advice on Equipment and Helpful Hints

Cameras

Most cameras now use batteries for metering the light and for film transportation. As you will be taking many more photographs than usual and often in high temperatures, it is a good idea to bring along an extra battery. A high proportion of cameras also have auto-focus facility – these cameras can be particularly hard on batteries and therefore you must bring at least one spare battery even if you have started the safari with a new one in your camera. The keen camera enthusiast will want to bring along several lenses which can be bulky and heavy. A 28 mm–85 mm zoom lens and a 100 mm–300 mm zoom lens will cover most of your requirements, but if you want to specialize in birds a lens of at least 400 mm is a good idea. A second camera body is both useful and an insurance against unforeseen technical disasters!

When taking photographs from a vehicle, *insist* that the driver turns the engine off (even if you are only using a small lens). Use a bean bag; these are provided by only one or two top safari companies, so take your own. The cost is minimal, so it can be discarded at the end of the safari if luggage space is at a premium. If you are photographing from a mini-van, try to avoid the temptation of taking the photograph from the roof hatch. You will get a far better camera angle from lower down, through the open window.

Driving in the National Parks and Reserves can be very hot and dusty. While the safest place for your camera and lenses is in a well-padded camera bag, you will miss many photographic opportunities if it is kept there. A good idea is for it to be on your lap, covered by a towel or the ubiquitous *kikoi* (soft cotton African cloth, freely available everywhere. When washed after your safari, the *kikoi* will make a super present, so it will not be wasted!). Your camera should be switched on and ready to go.

Video cameras

An increasing number of people are bringing video cameras on safari. As with still cameras, make sure that the engine is off before you attempt to film and remember that every sound is being picked up by the camera microphone. Sound can add a new element and can be a big plus compared to conventional cameras, but beware of people speaking nearby and be particularly alert to the wind direction, the sound of which can completely spoil your work. Recharging video batteries can be a problem, especially if you are on a camping safari, so bring several spare batteries or, better still, a cable to enable your video to run directly from the vehicle cigarette lighter.

One final word: bring lots of film. If you are a camera buff, think of the highest number of films that you may use and double it! Film, if available, is very expensive in Africa and it is far better to have too much than too little.

Binoculars

Surprisingly, many people come on safari with either no binoculars or inadequate ones. Although good ones can be expensive, at times they are worth their weight in gold. It's not necessary to go for big magnification, i.e. 10×50 or 12×50, which tend to be large and heavy. Smaller magnification binoculars such as 8×40 or 7×35 are ideal. Another bad size is 20×40 which, although small, light and high-powered, is far from ideal. A good guide is to divide the larger number by the smaller number and the result should be between four and five, never less. The first figure represents magnification and the second light-gathering power, the latter being more important.

Bibliography

Amin, A. & Eames, J., *Insight Guide, Kenya,* APA Productions, Germany, 1985.

Britton, P. L., *Birds of East Africa,* EANHS, Nairobi, 1980.

Brown, L., *African Birds of Prey,* Collins, London, 1970.

Burton, R., *Bird Behaviour,* Granada, London, 1985.

Fry, C. H., *The Bee-eaters,* T. & A. D. Poyser, London, 1984.

Hancock, J. & Elliott, H., *Herons of the World,* London Editions, London, 1978.

Johnson, P., *As Free as a Bird,* Struik, Cape Town, 1976.

Karmali, J., *Birds of Africa,* Collins, London, 1980.

Lewis, J. & Pomeroy, D., *A Bird Atlas of Kenya,* Balkema, Rotterdam, 1989.

Mackworth-Praed, C. W. & Grant, C. H. B., *African Handbook of Birds,* Series 1, Vols. 1 & 2, Longmans, London, 1957; 1960.

Maclean, G. L., *Roberts' Birds of Southern Africa,* The John Voelcker Book Fund, Cape Town, 1985.

Moore, R., *Where to Watch Birds in Kenya,* Trans Africa Press, Nairobi, 1982.

Newman, K., *Birdlife in Southern Africa,* Purnell, Johannesburg, Cape Town, London, 1971.

Williams, J. G., *A Field Guide to the National Parks of East Africa,* Collins, London, 1967.

Index